Dear Bill

LETTERS TO DAD
1939 – 1945

the war years

WENDY HAMILTON
AND CATHERINE PAVLIK

FriesenPress

One Printers Way
Altona, MB R0G0B0
Canada

www.friesenpress.com

Compiled and Transcribed by Wendy Hamilton and Cathie Pavlik

Content Disclaimer of this Epistolary Novel
For authenticity, each letter of the compilation is transcribed as close as possible to how
the author wrote it. Remember, many of these letters were written going out the door,
or overseas during war; not intended to be read with a critical eye. May the content,
grammar, spelling and punctuation you notice, add to the charm of the time period within
it was written.
As many of the letters say: "excuse the scribble."

ISBN
978-1-03-911767-9 (Hardcover)
978-1-03-911766-2 (Paperback)
978-1-03-911768-6 (eBook)

1. BIOGRAPHY & AUTOBIOGRAPHY, PERSONAL MEMOIRS

Distributed to the trade by The Ingram Book Company

TABLE OF CONTENTS

FOREWORD

A few months before passing away in 2015, my Dad gave me a wooden box stuffed with letters addressed to him, saying, "Wendy, maybe you can do something with these one day."

The box sat in my basement collecting dust for a few years and then one week my granddaughter, Dani, came over and we got to talking about the letters in the box. Inspired by her curiosity, we began sifting and sorting through the letters, reading the odd one. I knew - or so I thought – what the general gist of the contents would be. My five siblings and I had been hearing stories about Dad's work at the Royal Bank in Chilliwack B.C. as well as his WWII service in Lethbridge, Alta. and Pat Bay, B.C. (where he met our Mother) for a long time, and, after all, we had lived next door to my grandparents' (subsequently aunts') home forever. What was there to learn?

Dani helped to organize all the letters chronologically, and initiated a timeline for events as they arose. As her eyesight limited her ability to read cursive writing, the project slowed; and left to my own devices I again put aside the box.

When COVID hit in March 2020, I had a lot of time on my hands – so I returned to the box and all of the letters that Dani had meticulously organized - wrapped in red ribbons, labelled with the specific year - and I began typing.

v

I thought perhaps I could get them done and give copies to my siblings for Christmas. By November I knew I had not only an unrealistic timeline, but also that there was so much more to this than I first reckoned; wisely I asked my sister Cathie to collaborate with me. She eagerly agreed and through her expert detective work, was able to find corroborating pictures and clippings and other correspondences, which entwined and enhanced the effects of the letters.

So, what began as merely a task (saving / recording these letters that obviously meant so much to Dad) soon transformed to a deeply meaningful, emotional involvement for my sister and myself. We were taken unawares by the impact these letters would have on us.

The unique aspect of the correspondences is that, unlike emails of today, Dad could not keep records of letters he sent, only the ones he received. Consequently, his voice is silent – allowing the full embrace of the musings of his friends and relatives.

As we transcribed the letters, Cath and I became increasingly captivated with each writer and their story. We found ourselves gaining precious and oft needed insights that surprisingly had present day ramifications. On occasion, we found ourselves wishing we could 'step in' and share the humour, have a chat, eat some cookies, have a twirl on the dance floor or provide comfort.

It's an honour to have had Dad's trust with these moments in the history of his life and now be able to share them.

Wendy

This book is dedicated to
The Three Pals – our cousins Donna, Miles, and Barry - your bond
lives on.

CHAPTER ONE
1939

May – Bill travels to Revelstoke, B.C. to see the arrival of the royal couple, King George VI and Queen Elizabeth on their tour across Canada.

On the cusp of his 21ˢᵗ birthday, Bill was transferred from his job as teller at the Royal Bank of Canada in Kelowna, B.C. to the RBC in Chilliwack, B.C. He left behind in Kelowna, his parents, two brothers, two sisters, two nephews and a niece.

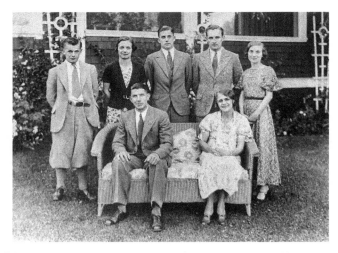

Photo of the Treadgold Family at home in the front yard on 1931 Abbott St. circa 1933.
Back: Bill, Frances, Jim, Jack, Wilma. Front: Arthur Thomas (Tom) and Sarah
Donalda (Don).

Home in Kelowna:

Front page of the Kelowna Daily Courier

GLOBAL EVENTS TIMELINE - 1939

May 17-June 15 - Royal Tour across Canada: King George VI and Queen Elizabeth – first ever Royal tour across Canada[i]

1 September - Germany invades Poland

3 September - Battle of the Atlantic begins

16 September - The Royal Canadian Navy escorted the first of hundreds of transatlantic convoys;[ii]

10 December - Canadian Infantry Division sails for Great Britain

Cited from https://www.mta.ca/library/courage/worldwariichronology.html

No. 635940 A.C.2

D.A. Chapman,

25 Squad "E" Flight

No 2 R.A.F. Dispatch

Cardington, Bedfordshire England

Mar. 14/39.

Dear Bill;

Well how is she hanging Willie? Sorry I haven't sent a line along to you before now but I just haven't had time. Boy I am dying for news of the old burg! I sure would like to know all about the basketball and how play-offs are going. I ought to be getting a letter from home pretty soon with some news of the events. I would give almost anything to have another nite on the floor with the whole gang. When you get away from Kelowna you realize what a swell joint it really is. I'm not homesick but I sure think of all the swell times I've had with you guys. Thanks again for your part in the Farewell supper you fellows gave me. I will never

3

forget that night and will always keep that case with me and the serviette with all the signatures on it.

Well, I have had a fairly eventful time since I left home. In New York the Colville Brothers, Alex Shibicky and Phil Watson of N.Y. Rangers showed us a good time. They took us to their apartment for supper and were going to bring over some dames and give us a "change of oil" but we didn't have time as we had to take our baggage to the boat.

Mac Colville, Neil Colville and Alex Shibicky, 1938.
All three are ranked in the 2009 book *100 Ranger Greats*.[iii]

On the boat we had a perfect time. We met the other five Canadians and one of them turned out to be Bill Hardman of Penticton who both Lawrence and I know. All of them were pretty swell mugs and one of them is still with Lawrence and I. There were four pretty good females on board that were worth looking at. There was a dance orchestra there which played every afternoon and nite and we taught the women to really swing it. There sure was a lot of beer floating around but of course I would never think of touching any. Larry got feeling pretty good a couple of times. I must say I like German beer. When we left the boat we left behind a few balling skirts but we were glad to get to England. The sea was fairly rough for quite a bit of the journey but I never got sick at all. England sure looked a dreary place when we landed, as it was drizzling rain, but an aunt of mine met me and brightened the situation. The Airforce gave us train tickets up to London and from there I abled home and went to my Aunt's. I met the other kids on Sunday and we looked over London and on Tuesday we signed up and left for camp. I have gone in for six years as a Wireless Operator. Right now the pay isn't so hot, but get everything found from grub to safes and so expenses are light. Larry and I with our Matrics [senior matriculation] ought to be able to work up pretty well in a couple of years. Anyway, we will apply for Overseas Service and see the world which is what I want to do even if I don't save any money.

Cardington, this camp I am at now, is quite a place. Here the R100 and R101 airships were built and the former crashed here. There are two gigan- tic (huge) hangars here which are now used for building and testing the balloons for the London Balloon Defense. They are hauling balloons around the skies all day and they sure look swell. Larry and I and one other Canadian from Victoria are still together. The others are spread around in camps somewhere in this foggy old England. We remain here for 10 weeks drill and discipline and then go to our training camps. I can't say I am in love with this climate or country but will get used to it in a while. At Easter we get a 5-day grant and half our fare paid to any part of England and return, so I will go to my Aunt for a good sleep in a soft bed. How goes everything with you back in that wild and woolly west? Are you still in the dog-house with Marg or is that all patched up? If you happen to be speaking to Myrtle Blatter don't forget to give her my love and also say "hello" to Marg for me. How is basketball going with your team? I don't think you ever will get a team while the big Swede is on it. Well I must say "au revoir" for now as it is time for another parade. By the way, what "State" are you in? I suppose you got over the border and left me behind. I'm still in Virginia (I think). Hope you are well and still enjoying life. Don't forget to drop a line sometime as letters are worth their weight in gold here.

As ever

Dave

W.G. Jaggard
O'BRIAN, BELL-IRVING, STONE, & ROOK, LTD
VANCOUVER BLOCK,
VANCOUVER, CANADA

Aug.11/39

Dear Jim and Bill.

Just a line hoping that you both have lost those lines of worry and anxiety by now. We all certainly had a wonderful trip and one to remember. If you have any good pictures of crews or finishes of races let me have them will you. If you know anyone who caught the finish of the #four race kindly forward same.

The trip home was pretty awful. Bayne drove Luca and myself to Penticton and from there we came home with Croston. Bayne staying at Penticton for a couple of days. Bayne had two flats on the way and we didn't arrive in Penticton until 6 o'clock. From there we drove all night and arrived home about 10 AM Sat. What a hell of a ride. I'm still suffering from 'exposure'. Don and I drank beer until 12 PM but all I got was a bloated belly and a leaking bladder. Well, so long boys you won't have to worry about boats and finances for another year

"Babs". J.

P.S. and thanks for your hospitality and sportsmanship. Remember us to the boys especially Iron Man Chapman.

The Kelowna Rowing Crew - 1938-39

Russ Scrim & Bill. Russ and Dad were friends through childhood.
Russ got Dad into the Royal Bank

Teenager Bill rowing on Okanagan Lake circa 1938

Bert, Harold, Dave and Art

Sarah Donalda Treadgold
Kelowna, B.C.

Sept. 27th, 1939

Dear Bill,

Your letters were both received to-day. Glad to hear you are fine and hope the daze is wearing off. Don't worry about 'The Cage' Bill as you will get on fine. We will be leaving here I think around the end of the week. We may take Jim's car, so will be calling on you sometime soon. I must get ready myself since I have been doing plums today. This is a busy time with fruit and hard to get away. I will have a look for your pipe. I will see that you get the papers each week. Sunday is Wilma's birthday. Jack and Jim got some ducks so we have been cooking a few but they are a bother.

I met Allan Cameron today and he wished to be remembered to you.

Most of the pigeons are gone. Frances gave them to the kids at School.

Jim has just said the Rattenbury's wanted someone to drive them to the coast. Dad phoned but they are not sure. Just leaves me to go, does not seem certain, but I would like to drive so I expect we will be driving.

The house seems very quiet but I have been kept busy so far.

Mr. Sidney Old died yesterday. Jack was coming over for supper to-night. Jim was in for a few minutes but has gone. I have very little news but may add some more before I post this.

Hope you are feeling your best.

Friday

Bill, we are leaving Kelowna for Vancouver on Sat. Sept.30th by West Summerland so will see you soon. Kettle Valley. Mailing you the paper to-day.

with my love

Mother

S.D. Treadgold

Kelowna, B.C

Oct. 2, 1939 Tuesday noon

Dear Bill

Well Bill it is time I was writing you again. I received your letter and hope you had a nice time at the dance. I intended writing you on Tuesday but was out in the garden for awhile and then got tired. The Murchisons moved yesterday so we are busy now getting it ready for the new people. I got your Insurance receipt having paid $10.22. What about the rest if is due on the 29th let me know by return mail.

The apples - I spoke to Harold and he will get a nice box. I asked for about 3 different kinds so I hope to have them sent this week and I have not seen Jim since I got your letter but will remind him - Harold is down the lake to day. I will have to write you again in a day or so as I must cut this short. Dad is looking for me to do something next door as he is varnishing floor, felt I did well to scribble you a line. It has been raining the last two days part of the time & a little now this a.m. but it is all gone & the sun is out again. It rained most of the day yesterday. I must get your pipe and send it on. Jack took it - Jim gave it to him out of the car, so I guess it is in the shop. I have been quite busy since getting back with one thing and another. Let me know about the insurance. I hope you are feeling your best. With heaps of love from us all and I will write you in a day or so.

Your Mother

Donalda Treadgold

S.D. Treadgold
Ailsa Lodge, 1020 Melville St.
Vancouver B.C.

Oct. 4, 1939

"The Lounge"

Dear Bill,

Well Bill I must get this off this a.m. We are staying at this place it is a block down from the Dental building. You can stay if you wish. We are having a good rest It is very nice and quiet. Quite a few Kelowna people here. Nora Simpson is here staying for a time as her mother is very ill and is only a matter of time. We went out to the Ludlows last night. Uncle Bill is going to have an operation for appendix to-day, I think. She is not living with Bruce Willis any more. Has not been for some months.

It has been raining all night and day so far but before that the weather was lovely. Dad had a slight cold but I think he feels better he was so tired.

I expect to be finished with the Dentist today providing things are alright. I surely hope so this time. I got your pyjamas and will look for the odd shirt. This place is quite easy to find. I will enclose a card giving the address. 1020 Melville St. - just a block down from the Dental building nearer to the water. Our room is 55 - so we will see you when you come and you can have a room here. It is very reasonable. I expect a letter from Frances today. I must mail this so you will receive it soon; may write you again if there is anything, I want you to know. Dad says to make up your mind about the suit whether to pick there or if you had time here or keep what you have. You will know what you like better than we do. Well, I guess this is all. Hoping to see you soon.

      With heaps of love,

          Mother

                      S.D. Treadgold
                      Kelowna, B.C.

          Monday Morn. Oct 16th 1939.

Dear Bill.

Your letter received this morn. Glad you are O.K. We are all fine and the weather is nice too. We have the furnace going slowly. I sent you the Courier. That was all I had to send as I did not see Small paper. Anyway, I think the news is in the one. By the way Bill I forgot to tell you, Frances paid for the shirts and I am enclosing $ for a pr. of braces so get them if you need them now. Thank Frances.

The Murchisons are moving some time soon. The end of the week or earlier.

I have not been up town much since I got back have been busy getting place back into shape again.

So, you think I will not have anything to do. Well, I guess I won't have quite so much so when your things need repair, shorts or anything just send them home - find the cheapest way.

I am going to mail this in the local mail box. The Kiddies were over last night. I asked Barry where Bill was and he said Chilliwack, so his memory is good. I think we will be sending some apples before long. It always seems a time to get things done.

Dad gave a lot of pigeons away but they came back after. The Safe Way seems different without the familiar faces.

That Parfait Tray that was in Walton's is in there. He said he would bring me the pillow one day. I washed this A.M., so keeping at it as usual. Dad he is a little bit busy too I guess before the winter sets in and then there's always some one moving. I will write you again soon. Different people have been asking for you so didn't think you are quite forgotten. I think this is all the news, but will give you more soon.

So, with heaps of love from us all

Your Mother

Donalda Treadgold

Excuse the terrible scribble. Jim has just come in and would like to know if you would like to have a couple pheasants. He will send them if you do.

W.S. Dawson
P.O. Box 802
Kelowna, B.C.

Oct.23, 1939

My dear Bill

It was very nice of you to write me a letter and enclose $2.00 receipt - here within. I have been laid off all this week with Tummy flu so have not had the inclination to write, got rid of it Friday and today feel ok again. Krasselt had the key and was getting the Coach boat stowed away. Chapman also wanted some of his "Glad rays". Dick Parkinson said if there was room the Aquatic would like to put in a couple of dingeys for the winter. The shell has been varnished and all squared off. The man who did the work said that the varnish was awfully good he bought a pint for himself.

Am sorry they work (you) so hard at the Bank - they should pay you enough to live on perhaps you will get more as you lived at home in Kelowna your salary here would be based on a lower rate than if you had been a stranger, so now you are a stranger in Chilliwack they ought to raise it up don't you think.

I don't suppose there are many places where so much goes on as in Kelowna where there is a club for almost everything. I hope you will join some congenial club in Chilliwack it will make it much more interesting for you.

Many thanks my wife is making slow progress.

All the best

Yours sincerely

W. Sydney Dawson

S.D. Treadgold
Kelowna

Oct 27/39

Dear Bill

Your letter received written after being in or around New Westminster. Well, we had quite a heavy fall of snow and so wet. It came Wed. night and I had to take it off the shrubs and trees. So heavy. A lot of it has gone and it is not cold so I guess it will all go. I am mailing the paper in todays mail so thought I would get this note off too. I told Harold to send the apples so I hope he gets them off at once which I expect he will do. I will give Theresa a ring. The shirt was from Frances, seeing you asked. Jim was going out yesterday morning to get your pheasants and it was snowing in the morning however—they will arrive sometime. We have been busy fixing up the house next door. Frances is having a few girls in for supper to-night. So, I am busy as usual getting things done. I hope to get a letter from you to-day. We are burning sawdust in the furnace. I think we will be for the winter as we have little wood this year. The new home at the back of our place is almost up. Mrs. Hampson told me I could go through her place so I will still have my short cut. We can leave a board off the fence next door. The new neighbours are good friends of the Hampsons.

Well, I must have my lunch, by the way I asked Jack about the pipe and he said he thought it came out of Bob Haldane's car. And I think he gave it to Jim. However, I told Jack to ask him and he said he would, so, there it is. I found a nice small shaft - pipe in a box here this morning - would that be any good? I think it was Jack's a long time ago as it was on the veranda with other things.

This is a 'great scribble' as usual but will let you know we are all fine and write soon with heaps of love

Your Mother

Don. Treadgold

Received your letter at noon. Sorry about your cold. I won't be very cheerful but you should have taken my bottle of Castor Oil Bill.

By the way don't worry about those crazy boys who like to drink so much. There are lots of nice men that don't in the world. Dad has just taken Frances to school. If you get a chance go into a nice private home for the winter Bill. I think it perhaps would be better, so think it over. It is very messy here under your feet.

I must mail this. I will put $$ in this to help with your insurance. It will get paid one of these days. And don't worry about those boys.

So with heaps of love

Mother

S.D. Treadgold
Kelowna, B.C.

Friday Nov. 3rd, 1939 Just before lunch

Dear Bill

Just a line to let you know we are still living and fine. I have been up town and back and lunch nearly ready so thought I would get a line off to you. Glad you received the apples. You want to know who paid for them? Well, don't worry about that as Harold got the apples and I paid for the sending of them at least, I expect to straighten it out with Wilma. She says they will send another kind later. Hope they are good. Well Bill if you are broke let me know I am not quite broke yet: You will know that best but you might get a nice place to stay and not cost quite so much and perhaps more comfortable, however suit yourself. Jim is away this week in the Caribou, I think Violet went home for the week. I expect Jim will soon be home. I may have told you that before. The weather is lovely today and drying up the muck.

Downtown Kelowna circa 1939

I have been sewing this week. Made Wilma a nice black coat - at least I hope it will be nice. Wilma got a lovely picture of the kiddies coloured. Very good. Would you like one?

I guess I had better end my letter. Write soon and let me know the news.

Hope you like your new suit as you wear it. Will write again soon sending the paper with this letter. Such a 'scribble' as usual. Where did you stay in Vancouver at night? I expect you will get the chance to have a ride. Write soon.

      With heaps of love

         Mother

S.D. Treadgold
Kelowna, B.C.

Thursday noon (Nov. 9, 1939) before lunch

Dear Bill

Well, it is time I was getting a line to you again. I received your letter written on Sunday last night. Well, I guess I have a surprise for you as I am going to Vancouver on Saturday night, Nov. 11th. This Saturday and will be in The Vancouver Hotel on Sunday morning. I am going K.V.R so will get in on the same train I guess as you did, but I guess not either as I don't believe it gets in until 11 o'clock.

I am going to the Trustees' Convention[iv]. It lasts two days so I will leave Vancouver Wednesday night and be home Thursday morning. I would like to see you there if you go to Vancouver for the weekend. I hope you can get a ride. Mr. Chapman and Mr. Shugg are going too. I will be busy getting done up again for a day or so. We have had a couple of days rain. Yesterday some wind to dry up the leaves etc.

Everything is as usual. Dad said he would find out about the bicycle to-day. I would have written the first of the week but waited for the school meeting to see if I would be going to the Coast - we had that last night. The paper comes out a day earlier but we have not had ours yet. Dad seems to forget.

Dad has just given me a dollar to put in this letter. If you are short, I will let you have some if I see you on Sunday. I am going to mail this across the way now so it will go in this mail. I leave Sat night on the Bus. Hope you are feeling fine.

With heaps of love Mother

S.D. Treadgold
Kelowna, B.C.

Tuesday Nov. 21st, 1939

Dear Bill

Received your letter yesterday and sorry the coat was a wee bit large. Perhaps the other one will fit better as it is only a 35 size. If it is too long, I expect it could be shortened. It is difficult to get things just right when not tried on, however I hope in the end you will be satisfied so let me know. I am going up town to mail this.

Glad to hear your office is getting on a better footing or in better shape. The weather is very nice but a little dark at times. One of the Wall girls (Hilda Wall) she is one of the twins died last night. She fell while on roller skates and developed blood poisoning - was not sick long. Frances says she is the nicest one of the family.

The boats around England are surely sinking these days. It seems terrible. The British will have to get busy and halt it.

Glad to hear you got your pheasants and hope you received your bicycle which Dad shipped.

There is very little news. We all manage to keep busy. Dad is fixing up his picture frame dept. This morning I had to do some shopping for the school. I have told them to write you so we will see what they do.

The town is collecting for the Red Cross these days I think they have between six and seven thousand over the weekend. I don't think they will get their objective $20,000.

I should be out in the garden to get all finished before the foul weather. I will write again this week. So, hope you are fine. Xmas will soon be here if wait seems long now.

So with lots of love

      Your Mother

      Don Treadgold

                  S.D. Treadgold
                  Kelowna, B.C.

          Sat. Nov. 25, 1939

Dear Bill,

Well Bill I must get a line off to you. It is just after noon. I wish you Many Happy Returns of your birthday. I am sending you a small box of cookies, candies, nothing very great but just thought I would like to send it. You will be sorry to hear of Bob Stillingfleet's death. It seems so sudden as you well knew he went over the bank going to McCullough. He will be buried tomorrow. The weather is rather foggy the last couple of nights so that may have been partly the cause. They did not find him for a time – at least a few hours.

Frances did not come in for lunch yet. The English Church bazaar is on to-day also last night but I did not see anything I wanted so bought very little.

Barry and Donna were over last night for a few minutes. They are growing up. I have very little news. I didn't go out a great lot but I am going up to mail this and my parcel. So, hope you enjoy the contents.

The weather is quite mild. Mrs. Stillingfleet was away but I think she got back yesterday. She has been on The Apple Tour.

Well Bill best of love

Your Mother

Hope you heard the Birthday broadcast. I sent it in but did not know whether you would hear it or not.

S.D. Treadgold.
Kelowna. B.C.

Tuesday Nov. 28/39.

Dear Bill,

Your letter received yesterday. Sorry you have not yet received your bicycle but it will arrive one of these days. I will enclose the bill for you. I think Dad was going to speak to them about it.

So they have spoken about taking off your salary for pension. What you should do is go to the manager in a businesslike way and tell him you cannot board and clothe yourself and pay insurance on your salary. Lay your cards on the table and if he can't give you any satisfaction write to headquarters.

As I understand it when you boys leave home, they usually get more so have an understanding. Put down on paper what you receive. After all, one has to live right and the bank should pay more for your responsible job. There must be a slip someplace and no one can say anything about having an understanding. It is only business. So I hope you have at least satisfaction.

The weather is fine not too cold. It is just about 10:30 so I got at my letter just a little earlier. There is very little news everything is as usual. The war situation does not look too good with the sinking of all these boats. Really things are terrible. When ever will it right itself?

I must get lunch now. I may have to go to a board meeting this afternoon so I will enclose the bill. Dad paid for it so you should have nothing to pay so write me soon.

With heaps of love

Your Mother

S.D. Treadgold
Kelowna. B.C.

Friday Noon (Dec. 1/39)

Dear Bill,

Your two last letters received this noon and so you did ask for more money. Well Bill don't do anything in too much of a hurry. But Frances says she will write you a letter and get if off on tonight's mail and give you some points as what to say if you should want to write to head office. It should be a very nice letter, not a nasty one saying you had spoken to the manager or they would just refer the letter back to the manager – anyway she will write you so then make up your own mind. Keep your head and don't worry about it as all is well that ends well.

It is just about one o'clock and I must get this off in the mail so as you will get it tomorrow. You would have to tell them you have been well trained and like your work to get anywhere as you well know.

The weather is fine not cold. I was making Xmas cakes this morning. Have the cakes baking now. Well write soon and look for a letter from Frances and then suit yourself as to whether you write or not.

    With Love

       Mother

                    FM Treadgold
                    Kelowna, B.C.

           Dec.1 1939 Friday 7 P.M.

Dear Bill:

What do you think of the enclosed letter?

If you apply formally to the head office for an increase in salary, they will probably just send the letter back to your Manager, but I don't think he could find fault with a letter like this as it is a "nice" letter - just asking for a rise in a nice way. (rise is the noun; most people say <u>raise</u> which is a verb.)

You will know where to apply - the supervisor I thought - but it might be someone else. I don't see how anyone could object to such a letter - but maybe I am not right. Do what you think best. Try not to "row" with anyone.

Must catch the mail.

Love

Frances

PS Do your best writing and use business paper - the Bank's

(Fran's Form letter)

Chilliwack, B.C.

Dec.3, 1939.

Mr._____

Supervisor, Royal Bank of Canada

_____ St.

Vancouver B.C.

Dear Sir:

In September of this year, I was transferred from the Kelowna branch of the Royal Bank of Canada to the branch at Chilliwack.

I understand that when a transfer is made there is usually an adjustment in salary. This was not so in my case. My salary is still $60 per month.

I have been with the Royal Bank three and a half years; in which time I have received valuable training. I work hard and like my work and now, at twenty-one years of age I should like to be entirely self-supporting.

You will understand that when living expenses, life insurance payments, and the usual salary deductions are taken from a $60 salary there is little or nothing left for clothing, recreation and incidentals.

I therefore formally apply for an increase in salary. I have already spoken to Mr._____, Manager of the Chilliwack branch.

Thanking you for your attention, and hoping that you will see fit to make an adjustment,

I am,

Yours faithfully,

William O. Treadgold

J.S. Treadgold
Box 62
Kelowna B.C.

Dec. 5/39

Dear Bill:

Just a line to let you know that we are still alive and kicking. I should have answered your letter before but you know how it is.

Hope the pheasants were O.K. There was a fair amount of lead in them no doubt "just my good shooting". I got my limit but no more, had good luck when I went out which wasn't often. I spent a week of the pheasant season in the Caribou hunting geese and moose but came home properly skunked. I went with Geo. Sproule, Ed Harvey and Ron Weeks, they wanted to hunt geese and I moose, so we came back with neither. Next time I will go for moose only. I was going to go up for moose with Dan Hill but couldn't get away the week that he went, and he came home with a dandy one. We had a good time anyway got in a little duck shooting.

The deer shooting has been pretty slow so far and it closes next Sun. No snow as yet and very mild and the deer are away back yet. I got one early in the season, a nice spike up at the "grey backs'' the only one in 2 days with six hunters. I also got a 2 point a couple of weeks ago at Deep Creek. Enough for the hunting, but I must say we all miss you this year.

Jack took the boat down to the point at the beginning of the duck season and it is still down there I guess its all right but I guess I had better get it up right away as ducks close to-day.

Bob Haldane did quite a bit of hunting this year, and he doesn't look too bad, but I believe his heart is giving trouble now, poor guy sure does have it tough.

We have decided to go up above Sandburg's cabin at "deep creek" on Sunday, on the new North Fork Road. It goes in 14 miles from the forks and should be a good place to hunt for the last day. "Teddy" was pretty good at putting up the birds this year, but got a little wild at the end of the season.

So you don't care for the banker's life down there, I can't say I blame you very much from all I've heard. I wouldn't work for the buggers five minutes. Don't take too much "guff" from them as that isn't the only job in the world, as they probably think. If I didn't get any more money than you get for the work you do, I sure wouldn't stick to it too long especially if I didn't intend to make a lifetime of banking. However, don't do anything "rash". Hope none of the farm girls have you tangled in their hop vines.

I tried to fix your handle bars but that post is awful soft and won't hold much. As for the key, it must have been broken off in shipment.

Keep away from "excess liccur" and write soon.

    Jim

CHAPTER TWO
1940

Bill received a letter from the Canadian National Defense to report in Vernon, B.C. for 30 days of army training.

After completing this training, Bill returned to his Chilliwack RBC position, transferred to the RBC in Vancouver (Hastings & Nanaimo) and submitted his name to the Air Force as he didn't want the Army (notes from interview of Bill by Cathie Pavlik 2008).

Vernon Basic Training Camp, Bill front row 1st left.

GLOBAL EVENTS TIMELINE - 1940

9 April - Germany attacks Denmark and Norway

11 April - Vancouver shipyards began to build corvettes and mine-sweepers for action in the Battle of the Atlantic

25 April - Quebec women get the vote

10 May - Churchill elected; Holland overrun. Belgium surrenders

4 June - The Miracle of Dunkirk – the evacuation on 338,226 allied troops from France via flotilla of 800 vessels

10 June - Italy declares war on Britain and France. Canada declares war on Italy

22 June - France surrenders to Germany

21 June - National Resources Mobilization – an initiative for more effective Canadian war effort in the wake of the stunning German victories in Belgium and France. June 21 Conscription Act passed – providing for the conscription of able-bodied men for home defence.[v]

19 July - Hitler ordered Great Britain to surrender

8 August - German Aircraft were shot down over Britain and by the 15th there were heavy dogfights above England. Aug. 18th the 'Hardest Day" The Battle of Britain began and involved regular air attacks by the Luftwaffe – German Air Force

7 September - Nightly German blitz on London begins

28 October - Italy invades Egypt and Greece

Cited from https://www.mta.ca/library/courage/worldwariichronology.html

W.G. Miller
Kelowna, B.C.
Feb.25/40

Dear Bill,

Glad to hear from you William. I've been meaning to write you ever since you left - but you know how it is!

Harold went to Vancouver on Thursday, and will be home tomorrow. The cannery convention is on, but I don't suppose he'll have time to look you up.

Barry is four years old now. His birthday was on the 22nd of February. I bought him a Tinker Toy and he certainly likes it. I guess you know what they are - just like Jim's Meccano set - but made of wood. You probably sold them in Spurriers.

As for birthdays com up William here they are:

March 1st - Violet

March 3rd- - Dad

March 14th - Jim

April 2nd- Grandpa

April 10th - Jack

June 7th- Mother

October 17th- Frances

Nov 27th - your own

I think Allison's birthday is on March 6th, but I'm not quite sure.

How is the fellow in the Bank who takes deep breaths all the time? I got quite a kick out of that letter of yours.

The Oilers beat Kamloops 97-54, last night, at the Scout Hall. Imagine getting 97 points.

When are your holidays coming up? It will be nice to have you home for 3 weeks.

This is all for now,

Lots of love from all of us.

Wilma XXX

P.S Glad you like apples. Will send more if you let us know when you want them.

D. Chapman
10 Oakdene Rd.
Redhill, Sunny England[vi]

Mar 17/40.

Dear Bill:

Many thanks for your letter, no joking it sure
was swell to hear from you. My apologies in taking
so long to reply but I guess letter writing just
isn't one of my strong points. Well, there's so
much to say and tell you of that I'm buggered if
I know where to start. Glad to hear you got home
over Christmas time and enjoyed it, short as it
was. Phil wrote and said you were with him awhile.
So, you finally got shifted from Kelowna. Kind of
tough to leave the old Burg but better for you
in the end to tough out on your own. Now you're
settled, how do you like mil., Runty?

Well, you asked me so many questions I shouldn't
find it hard to fill a letter up. Not once have
I regretted coming over here, for I've had one
swell time since the day I landed. I've been kind
of lucky for Larry and I have gone everywhere
together in the Air Force and right now are still
together. At the moment we are up in Norfolk and
working in the East Coast Fight Command[vii]. Won't
say much about our work but it is very interesting and at times it's a bit exciting. From over
there you must think the war a very dead affair
but we see a fair bit of action although it never
gets in the papers. I know a few fellows, Wireless
operators[viii], who were over on a raid and didn't
get back but that is bound to happen in a war. The
other nite I was up on a nice grassy hill with

a very charming young lady and we watched the search lites and A.A. guns in action. Really it was quite impressive, especially with the 'goil friend' getting a bit scared.

Since being over here I've travelled around quite a bit and seen a fair amount of the country. I was stationed in the south of England near Bristol, for awhile and then I played on the Station R.A.F. Baseball Team. Every week we travelled somewhere and played and boy we had a swell team composed entirely of Canadians and we cleaned up every English team we met - Hot stuff! While at their camp we had 17 days dry leave. Larry and I and another kid rented a car and went to Scotland.

Boy is that some place and the women! Whoa! Did I meet some honeys! Going back this summer to see one special one. Guess I'm still as bad as ever, chasing the bits of "feminine charm". I've still got a soft spot for the Canadian girls but these dames have plenty on the ball! Afraid I'm not as "good" as I used to be but don't mind admitting it, for when over here with a war on you live each day, not for the future. I nibble a bit off fairly regular and must say it is kind of nice. I've been in London several times on leave and know my way around a few places. When there I've got a married dame I can stay with and boy is she a dream come true. I go with several different ones up in this part of the country but you know the old saying "safety in numbers". By the way, how are you doing with the fair sex? Don't say you're still crossing the border Virginie! Remember! What happened to May back in Kelowna, give her up!

Thanks also for the 2 snaps Bill, they sure are slick. I'm enclosing a snap of Larry and I taken a month or so ago. We wear civvies now and then for comfort and thus the scruffy attire. Don't you think we are affectionate pals! Sometime when I have a snap taken in uniform I'll send it along to you.

I hear from a few of the kids back home and so along with the Courier I keep up on the local scandal. Phil usually tells me who has married who and why. Sorry to hear that the basketball Ass. had to disband but I guess hockey is coming to the fore now. Every Sunday nite they broadcast, over here, the game that was played at Toronto on the Sat. nite and boy is it swell to once again hear Foster's voice - the boys tearing at it. Speaking of skating I've done quite a bit this winter for it was very cold here in Norfolk and boy did we like it. These pom English thought the weather was terrible and also thought we were nuts because we liked it. The address I've used is a civvy one which all my overseas mail comes thru for we aren't allowed to have overseas mail go direct to our service address. Please excuse this long note paper but as I can't find my pad I'm using this government stuff.

All Christmas time Larry and I were on duty but made up for that when we got to London on leave over the New Year. So we painted the joint red and gave a few gals a rough time. Some fun in London in the black outs, more than once I wound up in somebody's back alley. Everywhere I went I met Canadians and boy were the "skirts" going for them in a big way. I met 2 guys from Vernon and so we went out on a tear. Haven't met any from Kel. yet but maybe will someday.

Next time you see Connie and Doug please remember me to them. Afraid I must finish off soon for I have to get on duty. Sorry I rambled along so bad but you know me. Hope you and the boys stay out of this mess until you have to come over. That'll be plenty soon enough. Lousy written I know but that's me all over. Hope all goes well with you and please drop a line sometime in the near future it is swell to hear from you. In the meantime, keep "it" in your pants!

As Ever,

    Your pal

        Dave

              A.T. Treadgold
              Kelowna, B.C.

              Sept. 20th 1940

<u>Dear Bill</u>

In answer to your application re position guaranteeing getting people up if they get down has been <u>some what</u> digested – and no doubt you will hear further on this matter.

<u>Weed out the Bull</u> sure Jack going away has made a big difference to me in more ways than one. I have asked quite a few of Jack's friends if he was dissatisfied with the shop or fed up with everything in general, well they all tell the same

story – that Jack was not sick of anything and that he made up his mind months ago he was joining if possible.

As you know I haven't paid much attention to Bank, Books or shop for a long time. I left pretty much everything to Jack and it seems hard to take over the reigns and start all over again – well to get used to all this. I have been cashing up and posting everyday to get used to things and I'm not doing too badly. We are not busy at present and that helps things a lot of course. Well I can't think of any more at this time but some time we might get more into details. As soon as we see how things are, for instance if Jack is away for a long time, I will have to make some arrangements or on the other hand if business goes up the stump – anyways its just one of the ups and downs that no one can figure.

      Love

          Dad

Excuse scribble

The whistle here just blew 5 o'c

                    A.J. Treadgold
                Shaughnessy Hospital

                      Dec 3 / 40

Dear Bill

Received your letter today and am sorry to disappoint you about this weekend. I am in quarantine in this bloody hospital and they tell us we won't be out until the 20th but we expect to be out before that. I was just about ready to come out and one of the boys got measles, so they took him out and immediately slapped a plaster on the door. There are 15 of us in this ward, only one other from the same outfit I am with, the others are from all the different regiments. It is pretty damn dull with nothing to do but sit around all day. We will all be nuts before long. I feel pretty well now, but lost a lot of weight, however I won't be long putting it back on leading this life. I will keep you posted as to when I get out of here and maybe we can arrange something, I hope. Should have a letter pay coming when I get out so maybe I will be able to give you an assist.

I believe I will be getting home for New Years, how about you? Well, there is no more news Bill so will sign off and write later. Hope you are well.

Regards

Jack

A.T. Treadgold

Kelowna, B.C.

16 Dec. 1940

Dear Bill;

Here's a bit of shorthand. I intended writing you before this, but I have been so busy, and will be glad when Christmas is over. But is practically finished the outside work, of course there will be something coming in to keep the business going but this time of the year is usually slack.

Well Bill to come to the point of you coming here, really there wouldn't be anything that I would like better but I have given this question considerable thought, which looks quite simple for the present time. For instance, I have thought for a long time the authorities might give Jack his discharge ticket. In fact, I don't know how he got in. I know of quite a lot of fellows that are as good as Jack and have been given the go by.

Now the picture as I see it is this, if the two of you are here, people would or might talk and you might be expected to enlist - and by holding out as you are at present, might be playing a better game - In the first place Bill, I really thought that Jack would have gone East weeks ago and of course he might go soon, but he will be home New Years and I will find out his intentions.

Perhaps you cannot see my views and if not, the question is open for discussion. In any event, if we are operating next spring and work comes in as per usual, it'll be too much for me. I have been working pretty near every Sunday and back at nights, and if I intend holding on to the outside Painting I will have to give it more attention than I have been doing,

So until I see or hear from you don't get too panicky but keep in your dugout.

Mom and I were wondering if it wouldn't be foolish for you to spend Christmas here, she thinks it costs too much for such a rush – in today and out tomorrow, anyway Bill its up to you. I have enclosed 15 Bucks and you can use it for any old thing you care to.

I hope you can make out my shorthand ___and I am going to write Jack the same NOW.

> Dad

Mom wants to know by Saturday if you are (staying or coming)

> (no envelope)

Hello Bill. Just a line from the Old _____ to say that the weather is very mild, no snow and it rained yesterday. Well I told Barry that he would have to fix up the Christmas tree this year so he is doing it – and I think he will make a pretty good job. We took Barry and Donna to the Hospital yesterday and had them vaxinated for Whooping Cough. They were both pretty sick last night but seem better tonight.

Well Bill we are still doing work, the two men who are on will be busy for about 2 or 3 weeks yet – after that I don't know and sometimes, I don't care - I have got kind of sick finding work for others.

We can still get material but it wouldn't surprise me that before 1942 is halfway through there will be a lot we won't be able to get - but why worry. Well, I am still on the waggon haven't smoked since 4 July but I sometimes feel like having one. I may get my teeth pulled and then I might fall off —

We have had quite a bit of Venison lately. I am rather sick of it. Jack and the bunch got one last Sunday and one the Sunday before - but more of us seem meat hungry.

What do you think of the <u>Butter Rationing</u>? I wish they would take over everything and Ration it.

I framed all and everything I had for the shop and have sold quite a lot of pictures but gee the Town seems dead.

Well I suppose Mother will give you all the news so no use me taking up too much valuable time.

Well here's hoping you have a <u>dam good</u> time for Xmas.

      Your Dad

          excuse scribble

A.J. Treadgold
Shaughnessy Hospital

Dec 19 / 40

Dear Bill

The quarantine was lifted today but 3 of us couldn't go, damn it. I have been in bed for the last week with one hell of a cold, but am feeling much better now. I will probably get out Monday if everything goes alright.

You had better not count on seeing me until I know definitely what I can do etc. You go ahead and make your plans and let me know them and if I can work anything I will. I'm afraid it won't be much of a Christmas. I will phone you on Tues. if I can, so leave word at the bank where you will be if you are out.

Well, I hope everything is going OK, and maybe we will be able to get together yet.

Regards

Jack

CHAPTER THREE
1941

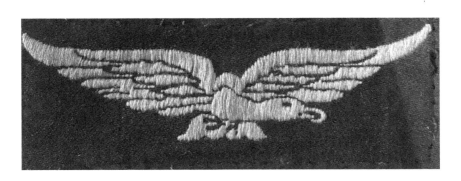

BILL'S TIMELINE - 1941

Bill transferred to the RBC in Vancouver (Hastings & Nanaimo) and at age 22 was accepted into the Air Force. He and another Kelowna local, Wally Meikle, travelled by train to Toronto joining up with 5000 other recruits at a big building that previously housed horses but was fixed up with bunk beds etc. to hold 5000 recruits. Bill had the top bunk. They were greeted at the building by three or four guys yelling "Sucker Sucker" because they had volunteered. He enjoyed Toronto because he got to see many of his relatives (aunts, uncles, cousins) there.

Manning Depot

After training, Bill was interviewed then posted to a brand-new station - Lethbridge: RCAF #4BG (bombing and gunnery) to both the Accounts (Pay Office) and Rationing Sections. There were six or eight of them. They had to pay 3,000 troops and figure how many rations each station needed, on a daily basis. They were paid $1.30 a day. When he got two stripes he made $2 a day (notes from interview of Bill by Cathie Pavlik, 2008).

GLOBAL EVENTS TIMELINE - 1941

Bombing Blitz against Britain's major cities continues

5 January - British invade Ethiopia and defeat Italian occupation

1 March - Bulgaria joined Axis

6 April - Germany invades Greece and Yugoslavia

13 April - Japan and Soviet Union sign a non-aggression pact

8 June – British and French forces invade Syria

22 June - German Invasion of Russia - Operation Barbarossa begins – advance was halted by severe weather

27 June - (Canada) Women allowed to enlist in army

7 December - Canada declares war on Romania

7 December - Japan attacks Pearl Harbor and the U.S. declares war on Japan as does Canada

8 December - Japan attacks Hong Kong's Kai Tak airport (the same morning as Pearl Harbor) – resulting in Battle of Hong Kong and the Fall of Hong Kong

https://www.mta.ca/library/courage/worldwariichronology.html cited May 28, 2021

W.G. Miller

Box 449

Kelowna, B.C.

Saturday March 15, 1941

Dear Bill,

Well, Jack and I arrived home this morning and the village certainly looks deserted. It seems so quiet - I believe I'd like to be back in Vancouver. So if I were you I'd think twice before quitting my job - I'd give it a fair trial, Bill; something else may turn up. I wouldn't join the Air Force if I were you - because we certainly wouldn't like to see you in that - not unless you join up as a bookkeeper in the Air Force - clerical work.

Your mother will be writing you just as soon as she can - please don't worry Bill - life's too short - and try to keep your chin up - it's a long road that has no turning, you know.

Please excuse the scribble because I want this to catch the mail out so you'll get it on Monday.

Barry and Donna are looking great - Barry is eating fine and by himself too! Wonders will never cease.

Please give my love to all the Ludlows and tell Aunty Nell and Uncle Bill I'll write them a line this week.

I have to take the children home now and get to work! Boy, oh boy!!! If you see Ella tell her I'll write this week too.

Mother seems to be glad I'm home - I guess the kids get on her nerves - saw the snaps you took in Vancouver - very good. Best regards to Jean.

Love from

Wilma xx

P.S. Hold on to your job for awhile now - don't be a quitter! Please.

I broke Jack's glasses (one (1) lens) on the train. Whatta life!!!

The Royal Bank of Canada
Chilliwack, B.C.
May 6 1941

Mr. William Treadgold,
% The Royal Bank of Canada,
Hastings & Nanaimo St., Br.,
Vancouver, B.C.

Dear Bill:

I have your letter of the 5th, and note your intentions of signing with the Air Force. I understand it is not the procedure of the managers to give letters of recommendation direct to officers, but I have much pleasure in forwarding one to the enlistment officer of the R.C.A. F. which I am doing to-day.

Wishing you success in obtaining the work you are after and with the best of luck, I am

Yours sincerely,

G.....C

Manager.

GC/PJR

P.S.

Very sorry to hear of Mr. Marsh's illness, and trust that his recovery will be speedy, and that he will soon be back to work.

The Royal Bank of Canada

Kelowna, B.C.,
May 6, 1941

Commanding Officer,
R.C.A.F.,
Recruiting Centre,
Vancouver, B.C.

Dear Sir:-

It has been my privilege to be intimately acquainted
with Mr. W. O. Treadgold during the past ten years,
and in that time I have formed a very high regard
for his many fine qualities. He is a young man of
genial disposition who enjoys an excellent reputa-
tion. He is industrious and I believe would put
forth every effort to make a success of any position which might be entrusted to him.

Yours truly,

F.T. Willis

Manager.

K-20 A.W. Krasselt
H.Q Squadron
9th Armoured Regt (BCD) CA.
Camp Borden[ix], Ont.

August 18, 1941

Dear Bill:

Received your very welcome letter the other day and
finally found time to answer it. We have been busy
as hell lately. In fact, I have had very few evenings off in the last six months. I guess you know

that I am working in the Quartermaster's stores and have been ever since I joined the outfit. We have had several big inspections lately, and as our books were months behind time, we just had to get down to work.

There is a lot of talk of us hopping the pond sometime within the next two months, but of course this is not definite.

The Regiment hasn't done a hell of a lot of training since we have been here. About half of the boys have been away on courses, and the rest have been f----- -- around with about 15 old 1919 American Tanks. We expect to get most of the tank training when we get overseas as it doesn't look as though we will get any modern equipment here. Enough about that.

I have been down to Toronto twice, and once to see Marguerite Bowes when she was out on her holidays and of course last week when the talks were there. Our weekends are from 5 o'clock Friday evening 'till 2 o'clock in the morning, Monday. We are allowed two of these per month. It is hard to take advantage of them as it costs quite a bit to make the trip.

The folks and I took the boat and went down to see Niagara Falls. They and the surrounding gardens and parks are really wonderful. I took several pictures, but was rather disappointed in them. The Boat trip was really swell. We danced on the boat to the music of different orchestras going and coming. This was quite a novelty especially when a guy was lucky enough to have a cute little number like I had. She was really a swell kid, in fact so swell, I am afraid that I will have to go to Toronto again to see her. I had an extra day's leave on that weekend and really enjoyed the three days break from the old routine of the Army.

We had a very enjoyable smoker last week to celebrate the forming of the Regiment a year ago. It was sure a rare evening. We drank about 280 gallons of beer, smoked hundreds of cigarettes, and plenty of crackers and cheese. It was sure hard to "hit the deck" at 6 o'clock the next morning. We all lived through it however.

I expect to get my furlough about the end of next month — am I ever looking forward to getting back to good old Kelowna — would have given my left __ to get home for Regatta. However, I guess the day will come. I was sure glad to hear that Alice Thompson kept Kelowna on the map again this year.

Well Bill, I sure wish you all the luck in the world when you get in the RCAF. It is too bad that we didn't all get into something together. However, I am hoping that sometime, we will all meet again and give Beaver Lake a dam good going over — that will be the day eh!

Can't think of anything more to say this time. Please remember me to anyone that you see, that I know.

So long, with best wished your Pal

Alban

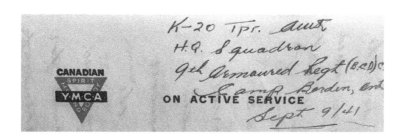

K-20 Tpr. Krasselt A.W.

HQ Squadron

9th Armoured Regt (B.C.D.)

Camp Borden, Ont.

Sept 9/41

Dear Bill:-

Thanks a lot for your welcome letter received last week. Hope that by now your cold has cleared up. I have had one myself but managed to live through it.

It looks very much as though our days are num-bered, here at Camp Borden. We are definitely going to move overseas in the near future. Dates etc. of course are strictly secret, but of course we have a good idea regarding them. The boys on the "advance party" are home on leave now and we expect embarkation leave to start quite soon for the whole Regiment. When this starts all furloughs are cancelled, and I was rather worried about mine, which is due on the 31st. I pulled a few "strings", however, and expect to get it starting the 15th. If so, it won't be long now. This will be my last trip home for a while I guess, so am really going to make the best of it. — Pin your ears back Kelowna for here I come —I hope. I will only get about 9 days at home, but that is better than 48 hours (embarkation leave) as it is one hell of a long way to go for that short of time.

I had a nice time in Toronto two weekends ago. Had one hell of a time to get a room though as it was Labour Day weekend, and the Exhibition was on. After walking and phoning all over the city, we managed to get a place to "hang our hat" in a boarding house. This wasn't handy as a hotel, but we made the best of it.

I had quite a wild time at a dance on Friday night and managed to get "home" about three. On Saturday afternoon I went out to the Exhibition. It was really a wonderful show. The crowds of course were terrific, and was it ever hot. I found that these inconveniences were worthwhile however. In the evening I had a date with Doreen. I met her after work and we took a moonlight cruise to Port Dalhousie and return. This is about a six-hour trip. We danced on deck all evening — what a time. I went out to the Park on Sunday afternoon and later to a concert at the Active Service Canteen.

When that was over, it was time to catch the bus for "Our little grey home in the East". Another weekend shot.

Doreen is quite a nice kid and one I would like to see more of, but as I may never see her again, I think of the song "It makes no difference now". I hear from her quite regularly though so — oh, you know me Bill "I have no use for the women".

Gosh Bill when it rains here, it really rains. It rained last night, and believe it or not we damn nearly had to swim to the mess hall for breakfast this morning.

Had better sign off now and make my bed before "lights out". Will enclose a snap of me that was taken in Toronto. Seems to me that you asked for one in your last letter.

So long Oscar with best wishes from

Your old chum

    Alban

                        A.Treadgold
                     Chilliwack BC

                        Sept 12/41

Dear Bill

Received your letter of the 31st and should have answered before. I received another letter from you a long time ago but there was no address on it so did not know where to write. Well Bill I am about the same as when you saw me last; cannot 'get' around very good and my hands are so damn crippled it is hard for me to write - so excuse this scribble. I get a letter from Jack every week. He is sure having good times, I have quite a lot of pictures he has sent on, also a medal that a lacrosse team that he was on, which won the championship of the school. Well Bill old boy I would

like to see you, they tell me you have no entice-
ments to bring you to Chilliwack any more but such
is life. Elmer Green's father called to see me a
while ago, he had Elmer's picture with him. Sorry
Bill you have got such a cold, take care of yourself good people are scarce. Well I will close for
this time. Come see me when you can,

I remain as ever your friend

'Dad' [Arthur/Grandfather]

S.D. Treadgold
Kelowna, B.C.

Sept 24th 1941

Dear Bill -

Your letter received and glad to hear you had a
nice weekend. I can't say we had anything extra
except we should be pleased. Wilma has improved
and hope it continues. She is at her home and
Madeline Poole is with her for the time being. She
and Madeline, Barry and Donna walked up town today
and looked fine. But this morning she was still on
the story here with me but she really is better I
think and she has started to do a little work. Dad
was over for a few minutes to night and he said she
said more to him than she has for weeks.

Thursday night

Well Bill I did not get this off so here goes
again Dad is working tonight but not me. Frances
is here doing lessons and I have both Donna and
Barry asleep.

Wilma, Harold, Barry, Donna

Harold and Wilma went to Penticton this afternoon will be back to-morrow. Wilma phoned about 11:30 and asked if I would keep Donna as she would like to go to Penticton so of course I said yes. She seemed a little better toward me. Madeline said she was off - no good this morning but by noon she seemed much better. A funny business. Anyway she came over for a hat about 2:30 and she looked pretty good. She said "this is a funny business. I have been through it before." I never said any-thing. I think what she means is that she really was through it before, then she had a relapse - which she does not understand as we have not told her yet. Of course, it may take time. It was quite a time coming on so may be a time completely going. She surely has been through a lot in her way, no wonder she can't understand. I hope she comes out of it soon and stays out. I think we will be keeping Barry for awhile - until we are sure. It has been such a worry at times. Frances got a couple of books from the library on mental cases. So we are reading - even Dad will soon know all about it. I intended writing sooner but goodness it was difficult to say anything definite. I will be glad when I feel my old self again and can think freely. I don't really worry but still it is hard. I will write Aunty Millie one of these days when I can write decently.

I have been uptown for a minute but not enough to do much shopping. It is a good thing I had my school work done or it would have been out of luck. Isobel and Betty left last night for Vancouver on the line. I hope you are fine. Dad heard to-day from a business man of Vernon that all the soldiers were leaving Vernon soon and there would be first training there so perhaps that is right.

I guess this is all for now.

    With my love

        Mother

                    Sept 30th Tuesday noon

Dear Bill,

Well Bill you will think me terrible — but really I mean well. I wrote you and never posted it - every day I mean to add more but with Wilma it has been a bit too much. I think she is better for keeps. I hope. Not all better yet. We get a girl over there to-day so I hope she proves good. She looks as if she can work. Comes from around Nelson. I have been over there some so as not to leave her alone. She still is not too good to me at times but she is doing a little work. That is all I can say. I am afraid to say too much as the picture changes so much. I was so sorry not to get my letter off yesterday but it is so easy to forget until mail time is over when someone phones for me but I hope we are on the upward path. Barry is still with me and I have not been uptown to do anything much yet. Dad wants your bicycle so don't sell it. He told me to tell you, so ship it when you are through. The weather is nice after some rain.

We have been wondering when you are coming this way. Dad is going to mail this for me.

Women's help has been so hard to get here - they are all in the canneries. Everybody else is fine. To-morrow is Wilma's birthday. Albert Krasselt called on me the day he left. He said he had been talking to you. It was very good of him to drop in on me. I think I will dress up to-day and take a walk. My nerves are half shot at times too but I am not going to let it get me - at least I hope not.

Well Bill don't be mad. I keep saying my letter should go but between one thing and another it has been a fright.

Hope you are feeling your best

    With my love

        Mother

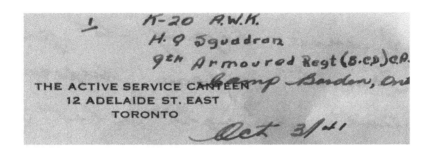

K-20 Tpr. A.W. Krasselt

H.Q. Squadron

9th Armoured Regt (B.C.D.) C.A.

Camp Borden Ont.

Oct.3/41

Dear Oscar:-

God kid here I am on "leave" again. Guess you will think that the army is all "leaves".

I just arrived back in Camp on Monday when a guy asked me where I wanted to go on "embarkation leave". I nearly dropped dead as they told me I wouldn't get any as my furlough was so close. However, they gave me 48 hours from the time I left camp, so here I am. I was hoping to get into Toronto again before I left but thought that my chances were nil.

The girl I met here when the folks were down is quite a nice kid. Her name is Doreen. I called her up when I arrived last night, and went up to her place for the evening. She was entertaining <u>five</u> other girls, and with her mother and herself I found myself surrounded with good looking girls. Too bad you weren't there!! Her mother is a singer of no mean ability and entertained us most of the evening that way. We really had a swell time. Doreen thought that I might be bashful and was rather worried about asking me up. She found out different as you would know. <u>Quit your boasting Krasselt</u>. We were out to dinner today, and am going a dancing tonight so it looks like a very nice holiday.

Guess you will wonder why I am wasting time writing letters while on leave. Here is the story. It is raining like hell out, and I felt that I should have written to you sooner thanking you for the much-appreciated phone call. It was really swell of you kid to give me a ring!!! <u>Thanks a million</u>.

Would have liked to have seen you again before I left, but don't forget Bill we will all get together again "sometime"—I hope.

We expect to leave soon, but if you address my mail to Borden, it will be forwarded. You might not hear from me for a while as you can understand. However, I will write as soon as possible after we get there, and will always keep you posted as to my address.

Might say that the night you phoned, all the family was home for supper, also Mrs. Chapman. I remembered you to them all, and they returned their best wishes. It was too bad that Elsie and I couldn't have been home together, but I guess it just wasn't meant to be.

Had better close now Bill and get cleaned up for tonight.

Will say au revoir, but not good-by wishing you all the luck in the world William, from your pal and buddy

Krass

P.S. If you see Eldith, remember me to her and give her my love. K

S.D. Treadgold
Kelowna, B.C.

Oct 9th 1941

Dear Bill

Your letter received yesterday and as usual glad to receive it. Well Bill I think I have a little better news this time. Wilma seemed quite a lot better yesterday. She and Donna went down to Oliver with Harold so hope she is still better when she returns around six o'clock to-night. Sometimes I think these trips are not good but still that is the way it goes. I advertised and was able to get a very good woman to look after her and every thing there, so that lets me out so much - Mrs. Caswell from Vancouver, (Jimmy Douglas' Mother-in-law). She is wonderful - so that should help a lot. She is a sister to Mrs. McCarthy and is here in Kelowna for the winter. She told me Wilma was much better yesterday - took more interest. I think the course is a zig zag one but I hope she is right this time. Wilma had a Russian girl so I have taken her here for a while, so I will have a rest and get settled again. I am feeling fine but it has been a worry. You can't help it. It is such a horrible illness. Although I try not to, but at times it sort of gets you. With having good help should make a difference.

I am glad you are fine and had a nice weekend. We have had some more rain. I think Dad is going to Vernon to Bowl to-day.

Barry is with us all the time, both he and Miles are going to Kindergarten in the morning and they like it. Mr. Gaddes takes them and Mrs. Ladd brings them home. Dad will take his turn when necessary. I have all the Couriers. I thought you would be home so did not send them.

I must drop a line to the Ludlows. It is just 9:30 I am at it early.

Everything is as usual. Frances is getting ready for a convention here next week. Harold Burr has been in town for a visit also Cliff Davis. Dad was speaking to them.

Well Bill, write soon. If I think of anything else I will add it later.

       With love

          Mother

                    S.D. Treadgold

                    Kelowna, B.C.

                    Oct. 21 / 41

Dear Bill

Well it is post time again and I have been think-ing of you. I received your letter last night, also last week's. I will enclose some cash. Well we are not too bad. Wilma's some better but at times she is still nervous. I have been there on and off since Sunday as the woman had to go home to nurse her husband again. I am advertising again to 'work on' for a woman for Wilma. They should be more plentiful soon as the packing lines will soon be through. I am sorry we could not keep the woman we had as she was very good with Wilma. I was over to-night for awhile and she seemed pretty good but it is a slow thing up and down — just time.

The election results are coming in and it seems as if Bennett (Conservative) has won here.[x]

The weather was nice today. Dad, Barry and I went out past Ellison to see a woman to-day. We enjoyed the trip and the roads are so good now.

Dad has gone to bed and Frances has come from Red Cross. We received your card and I got the socks and by the way there were two odd ones so if you have the others don't throw them away. I took my pad over to Wilma's expecting to get this letter written and off to-day. So, all your friends are gone. That is the way it goes. This has been a queer year for me. I have had to let the little things around home go sometimes but we are all still fine and that is the way it goes sometimes. Barry and Miles are still going to school so that helps me out quite a lot.

Jim has been getting some pheasants. He is busy making plugs. It seems he can sell lots as they are not coming from across the line. If they have enough pupils, he will be (teaching) school again. I expect it will be a couple of weeks or so before they know. Have many registered.

Dad has been busy doing signs. I think Bert leaves this weekend but I am not sure.

I think Grandpa will be going (back) before long.

I have not got very much news and the papers - I never know whether to send them or not, as I have been expecting you home all the time, by the way. I believe you asked me to send you a scarf. Well Bill I will finish this tomorrow. Hope you are fine.

To a Good night for now -

    Mother

                            Phil Chapman
                  L.A.C P.H.C., R92341,
            #7 S.F.T.S, Macleod, Alta.

                        Oct. ~~25~~ 24/41

Dear Ottley;

Many thanks for the letter received yesterday. I know you're a busy man and haven't much time.

Krassey told me you were going to Army Camp so I naturally figured that's where you were. When are you going?

It's now 6:45 A.M. and I'm sitting in the hangar doing nothing except try and keep warm. We used to fly at 8 in the morning but now we have to be here at 6:30 when on warnings. The last few days have been really nice and sunny with very little wind, but the nights are quite cool.

Yes, these crates are a bit bigger than the first ones we flew but after getting on to them are pretty nice to fly. I've been doing a lot of sitting around the last while which makes it that sometime I'll really have to start flying to get my time in. That's what I don't like, sitting around, and then later when time has to be up to date we're so rushed that we can't sit down at all. At times we all wish we didn't have to fly but if we were kicked out, would really be mad.

The ground course is quite heavy so I spend most of my nights trying to <u>learn </u>something and I'm telling you it's very little. Had "wings" parade for the graduating class and boy I sure wished it was me getting mine.

Have been to Calgary three times since I got here and hope to go again around the end of the month if I get a 36. The first two times I visited Eldith's relative in Calgary – not Edmonton and the third time a relative of Greensides. Its really a treat to get a little time off now and then so we can get out a bit.

So you've been seeing a little lacrosse lately, eh? To tell you the truth I didn't realize that lacrosse was even on now. Since I left home I don't seem to have had any summer. We all talk about "last summer" meaning the summer of 1940 as we seem to have missed it this year. We had hot weather but nothing like we usually had.

Ernie sure seems to have done pretty well for himself. I wouldn't mind a commission but as long as I get my wings I'll be happy. His mother was up to Kelowna a few days ago.

I saw in the paper that John Benmore got married. I guess you do alright now you have some women to work with in the office, eh?

Krassey said in one of his letters that you had phoned him and he sure sounded pleased. He seemed to have had a pretty good time while home on his leave. Sure wished I could have been home on my leave at the same time. The last letter I got from him said that things had changed and he didn't know when they would be going overseas.

This different writing is because of a new pen. It's now 7:30 in the evening and as I got interrupted this morning figured I had better get this finished now. Windy on a solo cross country to Huzzar and back which is about 200 miles and really enjoyed the trip as it was a swell day and not bumpy at all.

I think it's about time I got down to work. If I remember right you have a birthday around the 20th of this month. If it was this month I had better wish you the very best of everything. If it's next month, well, it still goes.

Behave yourself Ottley old man,

    Adios for now,

        Phil.

Phil - Bill

Alexander, E.A.
R.C.A.F OFFICERS' MESS
TRENTON ONT.

Nov. 23, 1941

Dear Bill,

I was both surprised and pleased to receive your letter from Toronto. Father told me that he had seen you off and I'm glad they had a chance to see you before you left.

When did you decide to join the service? What branch are you going into - aircrew or what?

Please write again and tell me all about what you are doing.

I just have a moment to write, but I thought you would be wanting to hear from me so I decided to drop you a line right away.

You are unlucky in not having someone you know with you. You will pro-bably get pretty lonely at times, but don't let it get you down.

You were lucky to be able to have a week at home. It sounds as though you had good sport hunting. Shooting a deer must be some fun. I never did any-thing like that so I don't know much about it, but it sounds damn good.

Brothers Ernie and Doug Alexander

Things here at Toronto go on in pretty much the same old dull fashion. Nothing of note happened since I saw you last. I just go on flying, messing about and really not accom-plishing very much, but there is nothing I can do about it so I mustn't beef too much.

I hope to get leave again in January and I shall go home and be married there. I get pretty fed up myself with this life and I should be much happier with Moira.

Doug is still at I.T.S [Initial Training School][xi] in Regina. He has been finished his course for about four weeks now, but they haven't posted him to an E.F.T.S [Elementary Flying Training School] as yet. He did well in his exams there and I hope he gets a break soon. He is playing a lot of bas-ketball in Regina and the R.C.A.F. team there with Doug and George Pringle playing have mopped up all opposition so far.

I'm keeping fit by playing squash every night before dinner. It is a fast, strenuous game and I enjoy it very much although I had never even played it before.

Well, I must be off to fly now, old boy, so I shall close. Please keep me posted on your movements and I hope we can see each other sometime – perhaps on a weekend in Toronto. Good luck, Bill, and keep your chin up.

As ever,

      your friend,

           Ernie

                      R.C.A.F OFFICERS' MESS
                              TRENTON ONT.

                              Dec. 22, 1941.

Dear Bill,

This will just be a short note to wish you a Merry Christmas and all my best wishes for the New Year. I'm sorry I haven't written you sooner but I can't seem to find a moment for letters these days. Also, I'm sorry I haven't seen you before now but that has been impossible. I have had one day off all this month. We are behind in our courses and all 48s and 38s were cancelled. It has been a tough grind this month and I'm nearly dead now. Thank goodness I'm off for 5 days starting tomorrow night. I'm going to Montreal to visit Mother's family there. It will be quite the holiday but that is what I need as I have had too long without a rest. I seem to have a run of dull students and bashing my brains out trying to put over the work is no fun.

I'm going home on Jan. 19th and hope to be married on the 24th. This will be a grim show, no doubt, but I suppose weddings have to be endured if one is to be married.

Mr. and Mrs. Chas. J. White

announce the marriage of their daughter

Moira Maitland

to

Flying Officer
Ernest Archibald Alexander
R.C.A.F.

on Saturday, the twenty-fourth day of January
nineteen hundred and forty-two
in West Point Grey United Church
Vancouver, British Columbia

At Home Trenton, Ontario
after February first

That is all for now. Bill. I hope to hear from you in the New Year and in the meantime, the best of luck to you. I hope you get posted soon as it must be poor waiting around. My sincere best wishes and Merry Christmas to you.

Your friend,

Ernie.

P.S. I'm a Flying Officer now as of the 15th of this month. I'm very pleased and it is a good Christmas present.

Ernie.

GTGVA291 5=NEWWESTMINSTER BC 24 355P=

R143019 AC 2 TREADGOLD W O=

3076RCAF MANNING DEPOT TOR=

LOVE AND BEST WISHES BILL=

JEANE..

CHAPTER FOUR
1942

Japanese aircraft sightings off B.C.'s Pacific Coast necessitated troops being transferred from Lethbridge to Pat Bay, B.C. Bill and his entire payroll office team (6-8) were transferred; Bill and the others found it odd that they were all being sent at once. The men arrived at the Pat Bay RCAF base under a shroud of scrutiny and each one was individually interrogated by civilian police. Unknown to all but one, money had been going missing from the Lethbridge base safe, and the RCAF superiors thought this approach best for finding the perpetrator. The guilty party, a Flight Sergeant, was found guilty and jailed for a year (notes from interview of Bill by Cathie Pavlik, 2008).

GLOBAL EVENTS TIMELINE - 1942

1 January - the term United Nations first used by President Roosevelt

2 January - Manilla falls to Japanese

13 January - advance by German submarines on North American shores – Operation Drumbeat begins[xii]

14 January - Internment of Japanese Canadians begins

8 February - Singapore falls to Japanese

27 February - Allies lose Battle of Java Sea

27 April - PM McKenzie King held a conscription ballot which passed

8 May - Allied victories at Coral Sea and Midway June 6 end Japanese advance

19 August - 3,367 Canadian casualties Dieppe

16 September - German forces enter Stalingrad in Russia

7-8 November – Allied forces land in North Africa – captured Tobruk from the Germans within 5 days

19 November Russians counter-attack Stalingrad

https://www.mta.ca/library/courage/worldwariichronology.html cited May 20 2021

Doug Monteith
CAN. R97951 LAC
ATTACHED RAF
RC OVERSEAS
4/1/42

Dear Bill,

I'm over here safe and sound. I'm damn sorry I
didn't see you before I left, but we'll meet
again soon.

I've been here about a week and like it very much.
This is a beautiful town. There are a hell of a lot
of houts [buildings made out of timber] here, most
of the troops are billeted in houts, we weren't so
lucky. We are in a Drill Hall which is about 1½
[miles] from the Mess Hall. I don't usually have
breakfast in the morning.

The meals here are swell. They are a bit better,
and more of it than I ever had in Canada.

The trip across was uneventful. We were on C deck,
16 men so a lot. The hammocks had to be strung
very close together. I slept very well consider-
ing everything. I hardly ever washed on the trip.
There were hardly any cans and half the time there
wasn't any water, salt or fresh. But we all survived. We didn't have any Christmas dinner this
year, maybe next year. Here's hoping.

At present I'm writing this, where I'm waiting for
some people to pick me up to take me to tea, some
relatives of Miss Dunn.

A couple of nights ago another fellow and I went to a First Aid Post party with one of Miss Dunn's cousins, I had a pretty fair time.

We attend 2 parades a day 9:00 and 2:00. Most of the time they only last for 1 hour or less, but yesterday we got screwed – we went on a route march and the god damned corporal got lost, we must have marched 7 or 8 miles before we finished.

We have a lot of time on our hands. I've been sight seeing around and going to shows.

The pubs here are nothing to write home about, the beer is lousy. They are open on Sundays though. They sell hard stuff when they can get it. It's too bad they don't have it that way in Canada.

There doesn't seem to be a hell of a lot of rationing, you can buy meals any time you like in cafes. I'm always eating. I'm beginning to become a tea granny. The coffee here is terrible it is made with an essence.

How's the Air Force coming along? I guess you'll be out of Manning Depot by the time you get this.

Write and let me know how you're doing. See you in London. Be good etc.

Love and kisses

Doug

"Keep in touch with the folks at home"

ON ACTIVE SERVICE
WITH THE
CANADIAN FORCES

K-20 Tpr. Krasselt A.W.

H.Q. Squadron,

9th Cdn. Armoured Regt. (B.C.D.)xiii

Canadian Army Overseas

Jan.13/42

Dear Bill,

Wish to hell that you were here to kick my pants for not answering your very welcome letter that I received some time ago, sooner. We have however been busy as hell since arriving here, and then of course I haven't got your Air Force address. However, I will send this to your home for forwarding.

Our trip over wasn't too bad although the grub and heating system were terrible. We slept in hammocks and must say that we had a lot of fun rolling each other out etc. The pond was quite calm with the exception of three or four days, when the old boat did its best to make us all sea sick. It didn't bother me, but some of the boys were quite sick. When we arrived over here, we were given an 8-hr train ride to the little town where we are at present billeted. I must say that conditions here are slightly differ-ent to those in Canada, but I don't mind it at all, in fact I am getting quite a kick out if it all.

I spent my five days 'landing leave' with relations in London who really showed me the "big town" and a very good time. I saw most places of interest and a lot of places that must have been very interesting before an egg or two dropped on them.

How do you like the R.C.A.F. Bill. Please drop me a line and tell me all about it. I want to know all about the gals that have come your way since you became a "little boy blue".

I got a letter from Phil the other day. I guess you know he is now a Sergeant Pilot and has an instructor's job, Nice going eh Bill?

Xmas and New Year were quite different this year to those I have been used to. We worked both days, and due to the fact that there were no lights or decorations over here, they just seemed like another couple of days to us. We had a big dinner on Sunday however, which included turkey, ham, sprouts, plum pudding etc. It sure tasted grand especially as the 'canks' didn't burn anything for a change.

The weather here has been really mild except for the last few days, when it has been quite cold. It has been raining, snowing, and blowing all day today so I guess winter came at last.

Closing now Bill, as it is time for "lights out". Hoping that you will forgive me for not writing sooner, and that you are "happy in the service".

Cheers, with best wishes and *Good Luck*.

Your pal,

    — I hope,

        Alban

A.T. Treadgold
Kelowna, B.C.

Friday night 7:50 (Feb. 6 1942)

Dear Bill

Well, everybody has to start to write the first one so here goes - and it will be in pencil as you can see. Mom has a school board meeting at the house tonight so I might as well give you the news. That is if I can think of anything as I go along. Cliff Bath was in town yesterday. I had lunch with him, he didn't know that Jim was in Vancouver so I gave him the address. Jim was going to call on Cliff but I suppose he has been busy. We had a letter from him today and I think he's still at the School.

Dug Kim is going to Vancouver next week and is to do War work so it looks like everybody and his dog will soon be away. Mom was just saying that she hasn't had a letter from you this week, that's tough. I just put Barry to bed, boy oh boy he is learning something new every day. Can almost read now, knows all his figures, letters etc.

We have had a few jobs in this last 2 weeks and have enough on for another two weeks for a couple of men but things have been extra quiet — perhaps Bert going to Vanc might be the best as far as he is concerned - looking ahead we might be very busy and we might be damned slack but I guess I can take it either.

In Jim's letter today he said that Grandpa got bumped down by a car and shook up a bit and that he was claiming damages from the Car owner who carried Insurance —

Mom told you that Mr. Palmer had died, well Mrs. Palmer died also and was buried today. I was a pallbearer — Mr. Cousins of Bankhead is to be buried tomorrow. George is working his store alone as both his men have joined up – he was saying today that he has had 5 funerals in 1 week. That's more than Edwards his undertaker had all last year.

Wilma's housekeeper has left and is going to her sister Mrs. McCarthy – Mom had a doz. applications but its hard to get anyone that's good.

Wilma is very quiet of late not much pep and is not eating very hearty, quite a worry it seems these mind sicknesses take a long time. I had read several Books on the mind and they all figure it takes a long time.

The weather is very mild no winter so far rainy yesterday and today no snow, no skating but I believe they are holding a ski tournament tomorrow while the chances are good.

I believe this has been the mildest winter we have ever had here, we haven't had any snow only an inch a couple of times and it has gone immediately.

I don't think that Bert is doing much at the coast. I have written him 2 letters and so far, I haven't had an answer.

As soon as the weather is good and mild, I think I will take a few days off and go and see Jim and perhaps I will take Wilma along for a change.

I have pretty much finished all the un-done things around here such as making drawers and I have a dandy meeting room where Grampa was. I dismantled

the room and have a small store and all the cupboards have doors and are all painted. Jack has
all the Jr. Board & Gyro side meeting there - but
if Grampa ever comes back, well I will have to
change over, but I don't expect that.

Jim was saying that Bill Ludlow has been very sick
again and they are thinking of an operation, well
at Bill's age its risky.

Well Bill I can't think of any more at present so
will say too to.

Dad

Tuesday evening

Dear Bill

Pencil as usual no drop, no blot — the news tonight
don't look so good for poor old Singapore in fact
the only news worthwhile seem to be what the
Russians are doing - it sure makes me laugh to read
the paper and hear the praises some or most of the
people give to them - the same people a year or
so ago couldn't think a bad enough name to call
them - we were sure given a bunch of lies - what
for - you can only guess.

Well we will owe you a Bicycle when you get back as
we are using yours. Jack rides home for dinner. I
intend to do the same later on — . We got started
on the day-light speed boat. When we get to the
shop its like 5 in the morning the only thing good
about it is we go home when its light and do a few
odd jobs etc. etc. Had a letter from Bert he is
making 93 1/2¢ per hr and he said that no one works

very hard when doing things for the Government. He is spray painting, what else I don't know, but I hope he sticks it out. We have 2 working but I believe things will be quiet — don't expect to see many new houses go up especially after the Government got all the money at the V. drive - it should be the D drive.

Frances is complaining that your Radio had a loud hum - and it is a little noise - did you ever notice it - let us know- and if no, I will have it tested. See by the paper that the EAST have had some storm, well the weather is mild here just like the end of March. Well I can't think of any more news, it's

no ink,
can't think,
some head,
to bed

        Dad

Kelowna Post Office circa 1940 - Ribelin photo

D. Monteith

No. 500 Squadron [xiv] RCAF Overseas.

10/2/42

Dear Bill,

How's everything going? I suppose you're hard at work at some cushy job at HQ. What a life and here I am out in the wilds, with F.A. to do with myself after working hours.

There are 4 of us with a corporal attached to another squadron on the station, although we still belong to 500. It's given me a better chance to learn this shit. As a matter of fact, I'm browned off already and don't give a damn, what happens.

You'll notice I'm writing a lot smaller, it's for economy's sake. The last month I've been going through writing paper like a dose of salt. It's hard to get now so I thought I'd cut down.

I'm supposed to be going on 3 ½ days leave a week on Friday. Bob McLaren, Joe McLeod and I are going to London and civilization. I think you met Bob in Vancouver on one of our beer parties. We are going to make the most of it by God.

One of the fellows in the room here is going to make a crayon sketch of Kay for me. It ought to be damn good. It will certainly be a nice thing to have as you can't have a sketch of your girl friend every day of the week.

By the way, how are you and the women getting along? Are you still getting into as much trouble ever? I bet you are, you can never keep out of trouble as far as women are concerned.

I was on duty crew and had to get up at 5:30 this morning. Boy what a change. I got off at 2:15 which was damn nice though. All I do at night is letters, read and eat. This goes on for months.

I'm sorry I can't write much of a letter but there's nothing to write about, every day's the same, Sundays included.

I've been pretty lucky. I've been getting mail from home pretty regularly. The last one was Dec. 31, they had received my cable that I was over here, which I was damn thankful to get.

I hope I will be hearing from you before long. No doubt I will because I know you're damn good with your writing.

Be good to the women

Doug

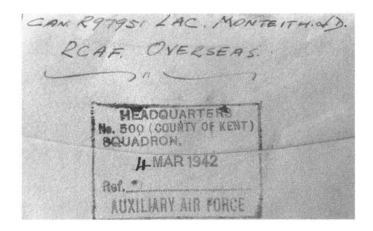

                                  D. Monteith
                   CAN. R97951 RCAF Overseas.
            No.500 Squadron, Auxiliary Airforce
                                        3/3/42

Dear Bill,

I got your letter the other day. I was damn glad
to hear from you.

Boy, I bet Lethbridge is all right. Any place would
be good news. At least there is some civilization
there. I imagine Earl is in about the same boat
as I'm in, as far as isolation goes. But you can
always get home from Coal Harbour.[xv]

I had 3½ days last month, 3 of us went to London
— Bob McLaren and Joe McLeod. I think you met
Bob sometime in the Devonshire probably (Is that
spelling right)

We stayed at the Duchy Hotel, for Canadian Troops
only - run by the K.C. It was darn good. 2/6 for
bed and breakfast. At each breakfast they gave you
a package of Exports. 3 beds to a room, with hot
water in each (room I mean) Just like an ordi-
nary hotel.

We were in and out of the Beaver Club quite a bit.
It's a central place for all Canadian Troops in
London – was quite a number of the boys who were
at UBC when I was.

We went to quite a few shows. But London's a big
place I think I'll go to a smaller town next leave.

I was standing at Piccadilly Circus when who should
walk by but Jack Edgar. He's a P.O. now. We had

85

lunch together and had quite a talk about the old town.

You seemed to have liked Toronto. I guess it was all right after you got settled. You didn't think much of it from your letters just after you'd arrived.

I hope you got my precious letter, I addressed it to Kelowna.

I'm really working – no kidding - usually work every night. I hate its bloody guts, no fooling. The sooner I get working on something won't be soon enough for me. But everything could be a lot worse. I'm beginning to realize what a fool I was to get into this trade. The life itself isn't too bad. You have a lot of fun and get around and see the world but it's the bloody work I do which I hate. I guess I'm cut out to be a pen pusher. I enjoyed it. How'd you feel about?

Don't think by my little speech that I'm in the dumps. Not on your life. 3½ days leave a month and 7 every 3 that's not too bad.

Did I tell you this before - forgive me if I did but you're just the same -remember Chuck? A fellow in the room made a sketch of Kay. It wasn't too bad at all. By the way the last letter I got from her told me that you had written. She told me the truth about you Billy.

I haven't heard from home or her for over 2 weeks. God knows what's happened to the mail.

Have you got a piece of fluff in Lethbridge yet? I bet you have you old devil. As for me I don't go for these bloody English women a bit. They gripe me. I haven't been out with a thing since I arrived. Don't think - I'll be thinking about Katy, and trying to remain loyal (that's not the word I mean but you get the idea. You know where I stand). But I don't go for them. I don't think much of the style of dancing here.

Well, I've said enough. I'll sign off. Write as often as you can. It really brightens up the old day getting word from the best part of the world.

Cheers and lots of luck

Doug

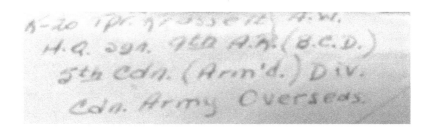

K-20 Tpr. Krasselt AW.
H.Q. Squadron 9th A.R. (B.C.D.)
5th Cdn. (Arm'd.) Div.
Cdn. Army Overseas

March 11/42

Dear Oscar:

Gosh kid was I ever pleased when I received your welcome letter today. Seems ages since I heard from you. I didn't write as I was waiting for your new address to arrive.

Don't know where in hell to start in this letter as I have forgotten what I told you in my last

87

letter. Hope you got it o.k. There really isn't a lot to say as since we have been camped "in the bush" since the middle of January I have only been to three dances and on one little 48 hr leave. The dances weren't so hot as this district has been pretty well "worked" by soldiers for the last couple of years. I spent my 48 hrs leave in London with relatives as I did my five-day landing leave. While there I went [to] a quite nice dance and spent one afternoon skating. I really enjoyed the latter and could go for a lot more of it. You know me. It sure seems a long time between our leaves over here. We are supposed to get a 48 hr and a seven day alternately every six weeks that gives us one of each, every three months. Hope you get what I mean. I am due for a seven day now, but as I am at present away from the regiment and attached to on Ordnance Unit[xvi] on a course I will have to wait 'till I get back, which will be in about five weeks. Am sure looking forward to it. The Course is on Ordnance Procedure, or at least it is supposed to be. However, after being here for two weeks I find that most of the time is spent trying to wear out the beautiful "square" they have here. They really are shooting the drill to us and after the day is over a guy doesn't feel like doing anything but going to bed. I don't really mind it though as it is quite a change for me. I don't get very much exercise at my usual job and have got soft as hell. I am feeling better now than I have for a long time and am eating like a horse.

I got a letter from Phil yesterday. The first that I have had from him in some time. They don't seem to be treating him so well in the East and he sure doesn't like the weather down there. Guess he will live through it though. I agree with you Bill re Phil going a long way in the Airforce, as he is the kind of guy that works like hell and I imagine that he would be pretty smart along that line. Wouldn't surprise me if he comes out of this mess with a commission. When I see the planes going over to drop a few eggs I wish to hell that I had transferred to the R.C.A.F. when I had the chance. I would have to, but my "call" didn't come through 'till we were ready to leave for overseas and I didn't have time to make arrangements. It is hard as hell to get a transfer out of the Armoured Div. anyway, but I sure would have made an attempt especially when they called me for a pilot.

The weather over here is unsettled as hell and a guy doesn't know what to expect next. Last week it snowed. It was just like spring over the weekend, and for the last two days it has been raining.

Don't know whether I could have trusted you with the gal friend in Toronto, but sure would have given you her address if I had known you were going to go there. I sure had a lot of fun in Toronto. It is quite a town. Would sure like to drop into the "Chicken Palace" or one of the "Honey Dew" cafés for a real feed again. From what I have seen over here their cafes and pubs can't compare with ours in Canada. Of course, this ration business doesn't help the situation. In London there are really some swell places to eat and drink, but in the districts and small towns they are just joints.

We had quite a nice time in the town we were billeted in when we first arrived. We were the first Canucks to hit the joint, and although at first the people weren't very friendly the situation improved considerably. Met quite a nice gal there and have an invitation to go back on leave. Don't know what to do about it as my relatives in London feel that I should go there on all my leaves. What a spot to be in. Would also like to go up to Scotland on leave as I hear that there are great things in store up there.

Will sign off now Bill as it is getting late. I did some laundry tonight and also cleaned all my ____scrubs. Still have to brush it all, clean boots and brass. What a life. Ha Ha. Hope you can read the worse than usual scribble, but as the writing room is closed tonight, I am writing this on my knee.

Cheerio, Bill. Wishing you the very best of luck and that I will hear from you again soon. Until then this is as ever

 Your Pal

 Krassy

P.S. Please remember me to any and all Kelowna guys you see in your travels. I'll do the same for you. Forgot to tell you that Mr. Harry Bowen and his son Leon were up to see us on Sunday. Leon just got out of hospital but like his Dad looking pretty well.

 Krassy

> #R110145,
> L.A.C. Alexander, W.D.,
> M.P.O #1303
> Macleod, Alta.
>
> Mar 21, 1942

Dear Bill,

I should have answered your letter sooner but we have been kept quite busy right along. I am getting lots of flying now and like it a lot. These Ansoms are not maneuverable like the Moths but there is lots to keep you busy flying accurately by instruments.

Ground school keeps me busy - the nights are taken up with studying usually. We have started night flying and that disrupts your sleep quite a bit. We have 18 hrs. to put in on that. Ernie and Moira are well settled now. I have only had one letter from each of them. Mum says Ernie doesn't write home very often now - I guess he finds enough to do without writing letters.

We get the odd 36 here. Last time I went to Calgary and enjoyed myself. I went out to #3S.F.T.S. at

Currie Barracks[xvii] and saw a lot of kids I knew. Also did a little flying in a Cessna.

It is going to be hard getting anywhere now that the busses have stopped running. I'll spend any other weekends I get off right here, I guess. I'd like to come to Lethbridge to see you Bill but its sort of difficult getting there. If I ever come, I'll try to get in touch with you though. It's hard to make arrangements because we are never sure when we'll get passes. They cancel them at the slightest provocation.

If you ever come here be sure and look me up. There isn't much here for entertainment but we could go to a show at least.

How are all your family, Bill? Mother, Dad & Sheila are all well. They had some R.A.F. (3) boys staying a week which was a good change for them.

I have to go on a flight now so will close. Hope you aren't working too hard and will get a promotion soon.

Best regards,

Doug

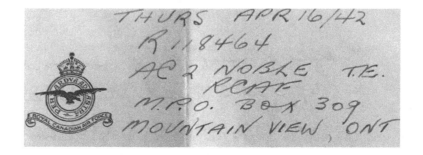

Noble, T.
R118464, AC2

April 16/42

Dear Bill;

Here I am again full of apologies for my tardiness
in answering your letter.

I passed the course okay at St Thomas and was
posted here at #6 Bombing and Gunnery School,
Mountain View Ont on March 18th. This is a fairly
new station, Bill, and the meals are swell and
there are no mess fees. We are situated about
125 east of Toronto on the shore of Lake Ontario
and are about 12 mi from Belleville which is the
closest town. All the airmen from Picton, Mountain
View, and Trenton, and Belleville I.T.S. [Initial
Training School] seem to congregate in Belleville
and all the fellows seem to have about the same
opinion of the place as you have about Lethbridge.
I haven't been into town as yet although I have
been here a month.

I was in Toronto about two weeks ago to see the
Ranger-Leaf game and it snowed for the two days
I was there. While I was there, I met Alvin Bowes
again and also saw Harold Burr who now has his commission as a flying instructor. I don't know where
he is stationed though.

You were asking me where Lyle Sanger is now. I
really don't know where he is now, Bill. The last I
heard about him was that he was home on sick leave
and though he might get his discharge. Harold
Sanger is in as a pilot and is probably finished

his training by now. Ralph Sanger has a commission in the B.C. Dragoons.

You mentioned that you get the Courier sent to you so I guess you read about Art MacDonald. Tough luck, eh Bill?

Have you any W.A.A.F.s [Women's Auxiliary Air Force] at Lethbridge? We have none here but a bunch of them will be coming here 1 June. We had them at St. Thomas and they sure were a crumby looking lot.

How did you make out on the trade test, Bill, and which grouping were you writing for? I will be writing for my "B" on Apr 26th so I have been doing a little studying lately. I am also taking a pre-entry aircrew course on this station and have been doing some studying along that line too, so I have really been a busy little lad lately.

We had a snowfall of about 3" one day last week and I could hardly believe it when I saw it. This eastern weather seems to leave a lot to be desired doesn't it?

Sorry to hear you had a session in the hospital, Bill. Here's hoping you didn't have to go in again. You sure are lucky to have met Doc Fumerton. When I was in Edmonton I met one of the Fumerton clan who worked in a clothing store there. I can't remember his name though.

Cripes, Bill! I can't think of any more B.S. to sling so I'll close for now. Here's hoping you find time to write again soon.

As ever,

Tom

Krasselt, A.W.
April 26/42

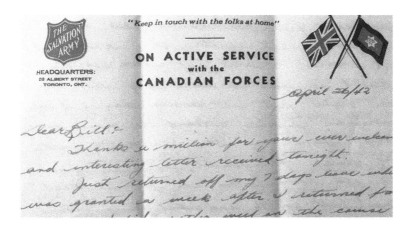

Dear Bill;

Thanks a million for your ever welcome and interesting letter received tonight.

Just returned off my 7 days leave which was granted
a week after I returned from course. I did rather
well on the course but sorry to say it won't benefit
me as far as promotion etc. goes in the Regt. as
the establishment doesn't call for it. Being away
was rather a break for me though and although they
kept me plenty busy at the school; I enjoyed it
quite well.

Was good and ready for my 7 days leave as it was
then two months overdue. We are supposed to get
one every three months but it just doesn't seem
to work out that way. Spent the first few days in
London and the latter in Bristol and Bath. While in
London I saw several shows, went dancing, boating
etc. I also tried to get in on the weekly broadcast
from the Beaver Club but was rather late getting

there so missed the chance — will try again sometime. Bristol is quite a nice city and although
the main part is badly damaged the surrounding
districts survived the ordeal very well. Spent one
day in Bath, with my cousin from Bristol, where
we saw the old Roman Baths, the famous Bath Abbey
(built in 676 and still going strong) etc.

The most outstanding show I saw in London was
stage play at the Adelphi Theatre. It was called
"Dancing Years" and starred Ivor Navello who also
composed all the music for the show as well as many
other popular hits. The singing and acting were
super which made it a really grand show.[xviii]

We had the pleasant surprise of a visit by the King
and Queen, which was paid to us last Friday. They
spoke to several boys whom of course were thrilled.

Received our Divisional "patches" last week. They
are maroon in colour with B.C.D. in red worked in
the centre. They look quite classy.

Speaking of my work Bill I am in the Q.M. stores
and do I ever get fed up with it. I was detailed
to the job when I joined the outfit and although
I have made several attempts to get out of it,
they all seem to be in vain. The guy who took
my place while I was away let things slip rather
badly so I will be due for lots of overtime. The
only extra pay I get is 25¢ per day "trades pay"
so you can see I won't be able to retire for some
time, especially as we only get half of our pay
while over here. The other half we will get when
it is all over that is of course if we are around
to collect it.

Like you (or at least like you say) I haven't been out with a woman other than my cousins for ages. Just don't get time. Guess my day will come though.

Yes, Oscar I get the local 'rag' quite regularly. Bill Riddell sends it to me. It sure makes good reading over here.

Will sign off for now as it is getting late and God knows I sure need my beauty sleep.

Cheerio, Bill — best of luck as always

    Krass

P.S. Please remember me to all Kelowna fellows you see. Thanks.

Crest of the B.C. Dragoons

P.H. CHAPMAN, #5E.F.T.S.,
HIGH RIVER.

29-4-42

Dear Ottley;

Many Thanks for the letter received a couple of days ago. It had been to Trenton and back to here.

Sneaked through my course at Trenton and I mean "sneaked" too. For some reason that place got me down and resulted in my flying being really terrible. They thought I couldn't fly at all but it was just that place. Was never so glad to get out of any place as I was to get out of Trenton.

Have been here for just over three weeks so am pretty well into the groove now. Was hoping to get here and was lucky. The part I like is that I'm only a day from home, also I'd sooner have western weather than the eastern stuff.

Saw Ernie and his better half a couple of days before I left. Was out to their place for supper one Sunday evening and enjoyed myself very much. Ernie works pretty hard but seems to like it there. I gave him your regards as you asked me too. Doug is at Macleod now, or probably you knew that already.

Bob Simpson was in the class that just graduated. I had the chance to fly with him but I don't like him much so didn't bother. He's no screamin' hell anyway.

Was figuring on getting into Calgary one of these days but so far haven't made it.

I tried like heck to get a place here so Eldith could come and live with me but I haven't had any luck. I think maybe she will be going to Kelowna but I'm not sure yet.

We are on leave from the Air Force while we are on this job and are classed as civilians. We have to have uniforms something like an officer's only it is dark blue, but I haven't got mine yet. We sleep two in a room and have a batman to clean our shoes etc. [A batman is a soldier or airman assigned to a commissioned officer as a personal servant.] We have our own mess but the meals aren't so hot.

We only work half a day but it's a long half and we really put in the time when we do work. Today we start at 2:30 pm and quit at 9 pm. Then have supper and to bed, starting again at 5 AM and fly until 11 AM. We are then off until 2:30 the next day, as we sort of work a day and then have a day off. When a guy eats at noon and then not until about 9:30 it is a darn long time.

So, you have found yourself another "goil"-friend eh? I thought you would, Ottley. I had an idea Jeanne was the one from Chilliwack but I thought that was all washed up a long time ago.

I imagine you passed your exams ok. Ottley, by the AC1. Nice going boy. Sorry to hear that you have to have your tonsils out. Hope you feel ok by the time you get this.

I saw Alvin Bowes when I was in Belleville one night and he was supposed to call me or drop me a line so we could make a date for the next weekend but he never did. It was easier for him to get hold of me than me to find him. If you write to him give him my regards please and also give him hell for me too.

Hope you make it home ok. It's a nice time of year to be there. Would sure like to go fishing in the lake myself. Maybe someday. I might get home around the end of June for a week.

Tuck was home I believe not long ago. He was in to see Ma. He wanted to re-muster to Air Crew but they found some little thing wrong with one eye. He was pretty disgusted when he was home as the choices they had given him weren't much better than G.D. I believe he is engaged to Barney Smith's sister. He was staying there.

When at Trenton we flew Harvards, Cessnas and Fleets which is like a Moth but here of course it's just an old "Tigerschmidt" (Tiger Moth). I'd like to have got on the Ferry Command [xvii] too but they thought differently.

The weather here on the whole has been pretty nice but it can blow to beat heck too. Have a few bad days every now and then. That seems to about bring me up to date now. Letters won't take long between us now. Hope you are enjoying life and everything is fine.

        Adios for now

            Phil

Sgt. Ward E.K.

Can R 118309

(attached RAF)

R.C.A.F Overseas

England

12/5/42

Dear Bill;

Sure is a long time since I last wrote you but I am hoping that you will make up for it with a prompt answer. Have been in England since the 22 of Mar. and in that time have had seven days leave, ten days with the army and spent the rest of the time at the reception depot.

Have been under R.A.F. officers but understand that we are to be put back under R.C.A.F. very soon. Don't know just how long it will be before I am on my course again.

Spent my Army Co-Op training with the 151 Con Div[xix] who have been over here for two years. They are the boys who rushed in for action and have been waiting ever since. Some are married and I met one with two children and an Eng. wife.

Expect to be on night bombers when I get there so, perhaps I will be seeing action before long. Have seen one or two enemy planes shot down and been in a few air-raids but it has been pretty quiet most of the time.

Met Cliff Davis, Joe Capozzi and Lionel Babcock since I have been here but have not been around to see any of the fellows who have been here longer. Met a couple of nice Scots lasses but the Eng. ones are a strange lot. Some of them are not too bad though and if you can treat them enough and tell them nothing you get along okay.

We are stationed at a lovely town on the sea shore and at this time of the year it is a wonder, to say the least. The parks and flowers are very beautiful. They also have a nice inside swimming pool here that is tops - 100' by 35' and 12' deep at the diving end. All white tile.

Haven't had any mail from home yet so don't know just what has been going on. I did hear from Thelma and she has a baby boy that arrived the day after I sailed.

Well Bill, this is all for this time. Please give my best to your family and don't forget to write me soon.

Bye for now

            Sincerely your pal

                Earl

Dear Bill:-

K-20 Tpr. Krasselt A.W.
K.Q. Sqn. 9th A.R. (B.C.D.)
5th Cdn. (Arm'd.) Div.
Cdn. Army Overseas

May 26, 1942

Dear Bill:-

Thanks for your very welcome letter received yesterday. I received an even dozen of them, and boy
is it ever nice when the mail from Canada rolls
in. The last one I received was from the Folks in
"Airmail" in which they enclosed a cutting from
the paper telling me the very sad news of Phil's
death. Gosh Kid did that ever throw me for a loop.
I still find it hard to believe as I had just
received a letter from him earlier in the day
telling me of his transfer to the West again, and
how much he was enjoying his new work. It sure will
be a blow to the Chapmans and I know that they
will take it hard as hell. It is also terrible for
Eldith and I sure feel sorry for her. She is sure

a swell girl. I guess that is how war goes though Bill, and there goes our good old foursome shot to hell. By the way do you ever hear from Russel Scrim. Would sure like to hear how the old so and so is doing and where he is now.

Guess you will remember a guy by the name of Frank Hawkey from Glenmore. He and I got rather browned off as the people over here would say which means fed up if you don't know, and went on a wild weekend to London the weekend before last. We both have relations there but we threw both them and caution to the side and really had a hell of a time. I had kind of a guilty conscience doing this as they would have felt quite hurt if they had known that I was in town and not gone to see them, however a guy feels kind of restricted when staying with relations, and we felt that we wanted to be free. Of course, I haven't mentioned this to the folks as they would also be mad as hell with me. We sure had a good time. On Saturday night, we went to the Hornsey Town Hall in the North end of London to dance. It is sure a swell joint. It has a spring floor and the orchestra is always super. The most important thing though is the swell bar they have up on a balcony in one end. We sure got feeling good, picked up a couple of gals and found our-selves about 8 miles from where we wanted to go at midnight. Of course, that doesn't sound very late to you, over there but all the dances start about 7 o'clock and the busses and tubes stop running about 11 so a guy just has to get home or near home pretty early. We were fortunate in stopping a cab which was going in our direction and finally made it home. We were supposed to meet the Gals on Sunday again but they failed to turn up. Frank and I weren't feeling very good anyway so decided to go back to camp. Our minds were changed though when we met another couple of gals on a tube and decided to go to Convent Gardens (guess you have heard of it) to dance. It is quite a classy place but was crowded as hell. A good time was had by all though and we seem to have made quite a hit with the gals. I got a letter from the one I was with during the week in which she enclosed a picture of herself. She is sure a nice- looking bit of stuff. Guess I will have to go to London again sometime.

Well Bill we have been over here just over seven months and by this time I should have had two 7-day and 2-48 hrs. leave. However, it just doesn't work that way and I have only had one of each with a weekend thrown in. They sure keep us plenty busy but I guess that is what we are here for.

Glad to hear that you are getting over your tonsil operation* O.K. and that you found a fair young lady with whom to pass your spare time.

Will sign off now Bill, hoping that you will excuse my feeble attempt at typing, it is easier to read than my writing though.

Best wishes and good luck to you Oscar, and write again soon. Until then this is it, as ever,

Your Pal

Krass

* Most harrowing time when I got my tonsils out in Lethbridge. I had a sore throat for 6 months prior - was in the hospital in Lethbridge for nearly 2 weeks. Penicillin hadn't been discovered. They thought I had mumps but I had strep throat (medical health officer sent him to hospital). Then was told

he had to get his tonsils out. We stood in line outside and when it was our turn we sat in the chair where the procedure was done. A specialist came in and we waited in alphabetical order. Shoved a big needle down my throat and gouged out my tonsils. There was 50 of us - blood everywhere. Allegedly, Bill's uvula was removed by mistake (notes from interview of Bill by Cathie Pavlik, 2008).

K-20 L/Cpl. Krasselt A.W.

H.Q. Sqn. 9th Arm'd Regt. (B.C.D.)

Cdn. Army Overseas

Aug.7/42

Dear Oscar:

Gosh kid it was sure swell to receive your very welcome letter yesterday dated July 1. It seemed ages since I heard from you last.

So, you don't like Pat Bay any too well eh? Might say Bill that Victoria and district seems to be a damn swell place when one looks back over the joints we have struck. We had a very good time while around there, however things might have changed by now.

So you have met the "one and only" at last eh Bill. Good luck to you kid and here's hoping everything turns out O.K. She must be a swell gal. Haven't any ideas along that line myself. Will have to look out though or will end up a Bachelor. Can't seem to get interested in any one gal. Guess I'm Jesus and love them all.

Can well imagine your feelings when visiting the Chapmans. It would be hell. I wrote them a line when I heard about it, but it was very short as I just didn't know what to say. Wrote Eldith a line at the same time. She sure is in a tough spot, but it would take a lot to get a gal like her down. Will drop her another line one of these days.

Have another 7-day leave coming up shortly. Think I'll give London a rest this time and head up North for a change. The boys seem to have a hell of a good time in Scotland, and I'd like to see that part of the country.

Have seen several Kelowna boys over here, other than those in the Regt. of course. They include: Len Richards, Hugh Kennedy, Jack Langley, Bill Embry, Art Hughes-Games, Benny Smith, The Bowers and several others. Bill Embry has certainly been around, and is very interesting to talk to.

Saw in the Local Rag that Bob Parfitt, Harold Pettman and others, have joined up lately. Kelowna must sure as hell be man free now.

Eric Chapman answered my last letter to Phil and sure made a swell job of it. Didn't think that Eric would take the time to write such a long and interesting letter. Sure appreciated it.

Will be taking up our beds and walking again shortly. This will make the fifth new place for me since I've been over here. Nice to get around though.

Haven't been out, other than to the odd show for ages, so haven't anything much in the way of news. Course there is lots but _____

Might say Bill that new orders out tell us to omit the "5th Cdn (Arm'd) Div" from our address as is on the back of the envelope. Thanking you please.

Will sign off now, as it is getting late.

Wishing you everything of the best, and hoping to hear from you again very soon.

Until then this is

    Best of Luck Pal,

       Krass

                Sgt. Ward E.K.
                Can. R 118309
        attached RAF - 214 Squad
           R.C.A.F Overseas

             August 8, 1942.

Dear Bill:

Sure glad to hear from you after such a long time. Things happen quickly in this Air Force and now I have fifteen trips over Germany to my credit and more or less know what it is like to be a gunner on one of our big bombers. Have been very lucky so far and although we have been shaken up a couple of times and had the kite looking like a sieve, none of our crew has been hit.

Have a Canadian Skipper (Vanc. man) Canadian Navigator, Scotch Wireless op. and front gunner, English rear gunner and engineer. I have done all my trips as mid-upper gunner. Jack Gibbs of Pent. is also on this squadron. He got married over here about two months ago.

Nice secure life you are living in the Air Force when you already have the future planned even as far as the lucky girl. She is most likely the first in a long line of prospective brides to be.

I am carrying on about the same, with one in every port and no sign of anything serious. At least not until after I finish my "ops".

Saw Harry Lawson a few times about a month ago and I have since heard of him through a friend of mine at another station.

Brother Bill is doing very well in his course but is not likely to be over here until after the new year. He will have a real course by that time - Wireless Observer with a commission, I hope.

Have had some good times in London, Scotland, Wales and been over most of the south of England.

These big kites are really beautiful to fly in and life is as thrilling as one could ask. Sometimes too much so. Long as my luck holds out I will do my hopo' in record time.[xx]

Well Bill I must close for now and I will be waiting for your answer.

My best to all the family

    Sincerely

        Earl

WENDY HAMILTON & CATHERINE PAVLIK

The Royal Bank of Canada
INCORPORATED 1869

Supervisor's Department

Vancouver, B.C.

October 6, 1942

Cpl. Treadgold, W.O.,
R 143019, R.C.A.F. Stn.,
Patricia Bay, B.C.

Dear Mr. Treadgold:-

With reference to your letter of October 3rd, as you are aware, the bank
made arrangements to pay single officers granted leave of absence for military
service an allowance which would ensure them two-thirds of the salary they were
receiving at the time they left the bank. Your salary was $950 per annum and
two-thirds of this amount is $633.33. At the time of your enlistment you received
$474.50 per annum from the Air Force, which meant that the bank paid you a monthly
allowance of $13.23. This sum was credited to your account at Kelowna branch each
month from December 15, 1941 to August 31st, 1942. However, you recently advised
us that on March 2nd your Air Force pay was increased to $602.25 per annum. On
July 1st it was increased to $730 per annum and on September 1st to $803 per annum.
From March 2nd, 1942 to July 1, 1942 your allowance was decreased to $2.59 per month
and from July 1st no allowance was applicable. The adjustment from March 2nd, 1942
to August 31st, 1942 amounted to $68.67, which was debited to your account at Kelowna.
We trust this will explain matters to your satisfaction.

Yours truly,

Staff Officer

Oct. 6/42

110

K-20 L/Cpl. Krasselt A.W.
H.Q. Sqn. 9th Arm'd Regt. (B.C.D.)
Cdn. Army Overseas

October 11, 1942

Dear Oscar:

Well you old so and so why for you not write for so
long? It's a nice thing when an old pal lets down.
On second thought Bill I won't be so tough with you
as maybe you didn't get my last letter, or maybe
the fishes are reading your reply, so I'll make
another attempt to get a few lines to you. Don't
quite know where to start as I've forgotten what I
told you last time. However, I think I covered my
trip to Scotland so will start from that.

Haven't had any leave since except for last weekend
which I spent visiting an old "flame" in Marlborough.
Really had a swell time too although it was very
short. Due to the fact that she is a farmer's
daughter and I stayed at their place, I really had
some grand grub. 'Course it wouldn't sound like
anything extra special to you over there, but it
was really a treat.

Since we have been here, we have had a weekly
Regimental dance, and are they ever good. It is held
in the NAAFI [Navy, Army and air force Institutes]
Canteen, and the music is supplied by an orchestra
from the 13 Light Field Ambulance [from Victoria].
Certainly is a treat to have the music played a la
Cdn. style for a change.

Expect another leave early next month and intend
spending half in Glasgow and half in London. Would
like to spend it all up North as I've got something

kinda "special" up there. However, I feel that I should see my relations again this time, so will spend a few days in London.

Except for one letter from Eric, I haven't heard a word from the Chapmans since Phil was killed. Guess I'll have to drop them another one of these days and see what's the holdup.

Went for a ten mile walk this afternoon. Guess that sounds funny to you, but I've really got to get in shape. Gosh Bill I've never been so soft in my life, and as I expect to have to do some special training soon, I've just got to do something about it. I realize that this is awfully short and that it's a terrible scribble but it seems to be all for this time, so will sign off.

Drop me a line soon Oscar and in the meantime, do as I do and keep it in your own pants.

Cheers, 'till next time with best wishes, and good luck

      Your Ol Pal

        Krass.

                K-20 L/Cpl. Krasselt A.W.

             H.Q. Sqn. 9th Arm'd Regt. (B.C.D.)

                   Cdn. Army Overseas

                       Oct. 25, 1942

Dear Bill:

Here I am again with a few lines in answer to your very welcome letter received a couple of days ago, and dated Sept 19. Certainly seemed a long time since I heard from you, but very glad I finally did.

Have been busy as hell changing scenery once more. Here we are in billets again. This time in a fair-sized city. Sure looks good too, and we should have a hell of a time here, that is of course while the money lasts. Was out for the first time last night, and attended a dance. Was it ever good, and the gals --- hold me back!!! Met Hugh McKenzie's oldest brother at the hop. He is a Captain with the 1st Div. Had quite a nice chat, although I'd never seen him before.

You certainly are a lucky kid to be able to go home on leave etc. Sure sounds good. What a day it will be if we ever get back there together. Sure nice to hear of some of the gang. They all seem to be going places, promotions seem very slow over here, especially along my line. You'd think that they were paying for them the way they hang on to stripes around here.

Gosh that Little Gal from Lethbridge seems to have you right where she wants you. Don't hear you kicking though so I guess you must like it. Won't be the same to see you wearing a "ball and chain".

Went in a weekend about a month ago to see a young lady I met when we first got our leave here. Really had a time too. Stayed with her people in the country and was treated like a king. Came home from the dance and as per usual found a bottle of stout and some ham sandwiches etc. waiting for me. Tea in bed in the morning and then a swell break-fast. Finished off a perfect dinner with some Xmas pudding (over a year old) that her mother had been saving for me all that time. Guess you wonder why all the talk about grub, but it really is a treat to get some good food for a change.

Can hardly wait for next Monday to roll around. Am going on another leave and this time for nine days. Due to travel conditions, they are combining our 48 and 7 day so here's hoping the money lasts. Expect to go to Glasgow first and then back to London. Will tell you all about it in my next letter.

Just took time out to take on a load of stew. Was going out tonight but the weather has changed my mind. It was swell out all day, but is now raining like H. so will stay in.

Seems to be all for now Oscar although I realize that this is a very poor attempt to exchange for your 10 page epistle. Will sign off anyway and try to do better in future. Until then this is, as ever

    Your Pal

      Krass

P.S. Don't forget to hang onto those stripes and add to them. I find the extra dough counts a lot.

      A.

K-20 L/Cpl. Krasselt A.W.

H.Q. Sqn. 9th Arm'd Regt. (B.C.D.)

Cdn. Army Overseas

Nov. 15, 1942

Hello Oscar:

Just returned from another very enjoyable leave spent in Glasgow and London. Will tell you all about it in my next letter.

Till then this is wishing you everything of the best and good luck.

Your Pal

Krass

ODE TO A CANADIAN

He'll ruin your life,
    And run off with your wife
And he'll think that he's doing no wrong.
    He'll take you around
If you'll lend him a pound
    And take all you have for a song.

He has a thousand mile ranch
    That was left him b y chance
At the death of his old Uncle Joss;
    He's a marvellous shot
And beleive it or not,
    He is a wonder at breaking a horse.

He'll gaze with a frown
    At old London town
And say "what a hell of a dump"
    Why back on the farm
It would go in the barn
    And then you go down with a thump.

He has personal charm
    That is meant to disarm
The unwary that come in his way,
    But don't listen to him
It's only a whim
    And surely will lead you astray.

Though you know he's a liar
    Your blood is on fire
When he whispers "L love you so much"
    You go weak at the knees
As he whispers "Oh Please"
    And you feel his experienced touch.

Though you may regret it
    You'll never forget it
Although it is breaking your heart
    To think of the kisses
That other young misses
May give him while you are apart.

Though he makes you so mad
    And quite often sad
Still you cannot send him away;
    He's a regular bad guy
With his roving hot eye
    But why do you whisper "Please stay".

He'll wed you of course
    When he gets his divorce
But while waiting, "Oh honey why not?"
    So just think of this
When he goes for a kiss
    (A PRAM costs a hell of a lot).

Included with Krass' Nov 15th letter

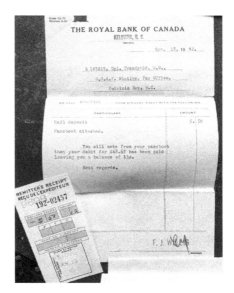

Royal Bank's remitter's receipt to Bill

> S.D. Treadgold
>
> Kelowna, B.C.
>
> Dec. 27th 42

Dear Bill –

Well it was good to hear your voice Bill and I am still wondering what you did all day. We were quiet and missed you all. We went to Wilma's for dinner at noon. Pat prepared the meal and it was very nice. They came here yesterday and I had Mr. Mims today for lunch. He was in town for a few days leaving tonight for Trail.

We went to Jack's for supper tonight so we have been on the go. Bob was up too. Bob gave me a nice set of Pyrex cooking dishes so I am quite set-up in that line. Very good of him indeed.

The kiddies had quite a full day with the usual gifts. To-day we have a lots of snow so the boys are in luck with their sleighs. Donna got a nice Panda bear, Doll, and both got skis, small ones and they like them so they are quite sports. Barry picked out a horse racing game and he loves that best of all, least he seems to, and a set of soldiers that will stand up. They liked all their things which were really very nice lucky kids.

Wilma went shopping by herself and did very well, chose things for the ones here and she seemed very good, then again, she lets herself sort of think. It looks as if it may take awhile.

Many thanks for your nice gift, Bill. I don't see how you make them*. Frances sent me a W.R.E.N.'s maple leaf brooch so it is nice too, I belong to both the Air Force and the Navy.

Jack and Alison went to the Mission to a dance last night and they all landed at Jack's after. He has a piano there now so they had quite a time. Jack seems to have a good time no matter where he is. He is looking better again.

Dad has a sore nerve in his hip to-day so he has gone to bed with the hot water bottle.

The weather is not cold but it looks like winter at the North Pole. I sent you the paper yesterday. Well, I will add a line to-morrow perhaps I'll be able to think of more.

Tuesday noon - well I have not got this off yet but will to-day. Received your letter written Xmas day. Glad you had as nice a day as you had but it would have been nice to be with you. I am wondering about you coming home. We have snow and if it keeps falling, I would not want you to have your truck somewhere in the hills but you will know what to do as it is rather risky. I don't know just when Dad may go down as he is feeling and looking better but the Dr. said he would be better to have his teeth out, so he will have to decide what he wants to do. I might go with him but now I just don't know. You surely were fortunate to have so many nice remembrances. I have not heard from Frances yet. She sent your socks but I have not opened the parcel it is done up so nicely but I would like to see them. We are all pretty good. Barry went home to see Donna to-day taking his sleigh and skis. I will have to look and see how to spell that word. He and Donna like skiing but Donna says it is hard work.

Miles was sick yesterday so is not out today,

I got a nice gift from Annie Gutpell yesterday - a silk slip. I am going to town this afternoon will write you again soon when I hear you will be home.

So be good and hope you enjoy 'The New Year's Day' and also a Happy New Year 1943.

So Bye Bye and Thanks for the long letter.

As ever,

Mother

*When Bill arrived at Pat Bay a fighter plane had crashed. Bill took some of the broken glass from the windshield and created small hearts. Wendy was given one of the beautifully crafted hearts, and during Sarah's funeral, knowing her Dad made it for her Granny, she snuck it into her casket.

Frances Muriel Treadgold proudly wearing her W.R.N.S. uniform

Sixteen B. C. Girls Join W:R.N.S.

Six prospective members o
Canadian Women's Naval Serv
ice entrained on Sunday nigh
for Galt, Ont., Naval Trainin;
School, to be sworn in on arriva
in Canada's senior service. An
additional group will leave nex
Sunday, their ranks to swell th(
total of western Canadian womer
who have enrolled in Vancouver

Those leaving on Sunday in
clude Miss N. M. S. Barrington
Miss Joan Ford, Miss M. T. Stev
ens Miss M. E. Whalen, all o:
Vancouver, and Miss A. E. Curti:
and Miss F. M. Treadgold o:
Kelowna.

Next week-end the list will in
clude Miss Diana Spencer, Miss
H. C. Booth, Miss C. A. Camp
bell, Miss G. S. McLaren, Miss
J. B. Forsyth, Miss J. R. Mennie,
Miss Margaret Paul, Miss N. M.
Ramsay and Miss M. I. Russell,
all of Vancouver, and Miss L. M.
Crane of New Westminster.

CHAPTER FIVE
1943

BILL'S TIMELINE - 1943

Bill remains stationed in Pat Bay, B.C.

GLOBAL EVENTS TIMELINE - 1943

2 February – The last German forces surrender Stalingrad

2-5 March – Allies defeated Japan's navy in Battle of the Bismarck Sea

13 May - Axis forces in Northern Africa surrender

July -August 17 – Allies invaded Sicily, forcing the withdrawal of German troops towards Messina; Canadians had suffered 2310 casualties including 562 deaths

10 July - British and Canadian troops occupy Italy

25 July - Mussolini voted out of power by his own Grand Council, Italy signs secret armistice

13 October - Italy declared war on Germany

20-28 December - 1372 Canadians die liberating Ortona,

Italy

https://www.mta.ca/library/courage/worldwariichronology.html cited May 29, 2021

S.D. Treadgold

Kelowna, B.C.

Jan. 3/43.

Dear Bill -

Well Bill we have real winter with snow. It is not so very cold but quite cool enough. I have just written Violet and Jim. I expect you saw them at the New Year. We were very quiet but Bob was here, also Wilma and we saw the old year out and the new one in, had a bottle of champagne and the house was nice and warm so we were quite at home. Wondering what you all were doing. We seem to get a little more snow every day. This is quite a scribble my hands are jerky to-night.

Barry has gone to bed. Dad and I are alone. Dad wrote a letter to Bert and he said it was hard work also to mind Gramps. I think we are all tired tonight but Barry does not want to go to sleep, with this daylight saving they have to be up in the dark. It is a fright for small children going to school so it won't be so grand in the morning.

Everywhere seems quiet – I will be glad when the winter has gone.

Dad is looking forward to cleaning up the shop, his place looks nice but it gets too dusty etc.

Jack went fishing on the lake to-day. Dad said three of them got small fish. It looks like the North Pole here with the snow – but we should not complain as it is not so cold.

I will send the paper on with this letter.

I intend dropping a line to the Fumertons so I will mention how pleased you were with your box.

Do you think you will be moved? Frances was in charge of one large building so she was busy. One of the girls was off for Xmas holidays. Then Frances went to Carillon Place for the New Year.

I have very little news Bill but I hope you enjoyed your 48. I don't know that I like it so quiet. It is nice to have a rest but there is such a thing as being too quiet. I don't need too much sleep. These days when the car is not used a great deal one stays put. I guess we are supposed to work and it is a good thing we can.

Tuesday – going to mail this now but before doing so will tell you of Elmer Green paying us a short visit. He passed through to Summerland at the New Year and came back yesterday and had supper with us. We enjoyed his visit; he is quite thin and although he has lost a lot of weight, he is feeling heaps better he says. He went up to Vernon last night and is going to Vancouver to-day by Bus or Truck or something of that sort. He said to tell you to drop a line to him.

We still have snow but not cold.

We would have liked to have had you for New Years but it's quite risky travelling as Elmer was 9 hrs late coming. Some days it is fine and on time. I will drop these in the mail box and write you again in a day or so.

So with heaps of love

      as ever

         Mother

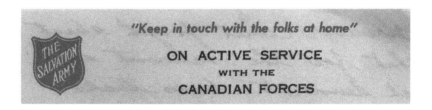

"Keep in touch with the folks at home"

ON ACTIVE SERVICE

WITH THE

CANADIAN FORCES

THE SALVATION ARMY

                    K-20 L/Cpl. Krasselt A.W.
          H.Q. Sqn. 9th Arm'd Regt. (B.C.D.)
                      Cdn. Army Overseas

                            Jan. 10, 1943

Dear Bill:

At last I've found a spare moment in which to answer your very welcome letter dated 21-11-42 and received on Xmas eve. Sorry Bill if you thought that I was bawling you out for not writing. Must have been in the wrong mood when I wrote that letter. Haven't been doing so well myself in regards to letter writing. Just don't get the time anymore and although it seems tough, and worries me quite a bit -- there is a war on -- so will have to attend to that first.

Several evenings each week are now taken up with additional training, route marches etc and believe me a guy is lucky if he gets time to take a crap. However, it isn't going to last forever so will grin and bear it.

Was last weekend ever a pleasant one. Had a letter from Joyce Chapman a week or so ago telling me that she had arrived over here, and as she was located quite close to London, she would like to meet me there sometime. I put in for a "weekend" and got it so phoned Joyce to tell her that I was coming. However, the "dope" who took the message got it all twisted, and when I phoned again from London Joyce was still wondering who had called her. As she was on duty then she couldn't come to London 'till Sunday morning. However, I visited with relations Saturday night and got up early Sunday morning and met Joyce at the Station. God, Bill you don't know how pleased I was to see her again. It was really swell to see a gal from Kelowna and spend the day with her. We didn't do anything very exciting but did we ever have a good chin wag. In the morning we visited several places of interest including Westminster Abbey, Parliament Buildings, walked across and under the new Waterloo Bridge, and also across Westminster Bridge etc. We then went to one of my Aunts for dinner, spent an hour or two dancing, back to my Aunt's for tea and then to the station. It was too bad that we couldn't have had Saturday night together as the time on Sunday really flew. However we hope to meet again sometime and really do things up right.

Saw Tim Armstrong at a local dance at Xmas -- or at least it was a "local" dance then. Didn't speak to him for very long as he was in a rush. He seems to be doing okay for himself and doesn't look much the worse for wear.

No Bill -- I'm not serious with any gal. The women over here are much too serious for my liking. If you take a gal to a dance she expects you to dance with her all night -- and thats no fun. If you take a girl out more than once she expects you to marry her -- and that seems a little too fast for yours truly. Of course, I have several good friends, but that's as far as it goes. 'Course one never knows the "right" young lady might turn up someday.

Had a very nice Xmas this year. An owner of a local stadium turned the place over to us for the day, with the result that we were able to have a Regimental dinner with all the boys eating at one sitting. He also let us use the dishes, cooking facilities, etc. in the place which added greatly to the meal. Very nice to put the mess tins to one side and eat off an honest to goodness plate for a change. The dinner itself consisted of turkey with all the trimmings including mince pies and Xmas pudding. As our cooks seemed to excel themselves in preparing it the dinner was rated as the best we have ever had in the army.

During the Festive Season I attended several swell dances and really had some good times. However, as we are now situated in the bush again, we won't be having the hall nor the time in which to really get out and swing it.

The weather here lately has been more true to the time of year than it has been. On Wednesday we had some snow (about 2 inches) however since then it has rained, thawed, frozen, etc. You can well imagine what a mess there is around here. Fortunately, we are all issued with rubber boots so can wade in the mud to our hearts content.

Thanks for Earl Ward's address. If I get time I'll drop him a line, as I'd really like to hear from him.

Yes Bill it really gets you when word comes through of Kelowna boys who are missing. However, that's war and who knows -- we might be next. God it certainly must be hell for their folks though.

Seems to be all for now Bill so will sign off. Please write again soon.

> Until then this is
> > As ever
>
> Your Pal Krass

Earl K Ward P/O J16074

Attached 214 Sqdn RAF
R.C.A.R. Overseas
11/1/43

Dear Bill:-

Received your Xmas letter and was more than pleased to hear from you again. Any news from home is welcome as what we do get is a bit old.

Vancouver seems so very far away but I often think of my friends and the good old days back in B.C. Went over to another station today and met Bill Wahl there. We were both surprised to see each other sitting at the dinner table in a strange mess.

I've met someone from Kelowna every time that I have been in London on leave which is quite often.

Jack Gibbs, who has been on the same squadron as I, has just finished his first tour of thirty "S.P."s. [shore patrols] and is on 4 days leave at present. He got married to a very swell girl a few months ago over here.

I still have a few trips to make but with a little luck I should be finished my tour in a couple of months. That sure will be the day and then I may try to get a pilot's course.

Received my Comm. on the 23rd of Oct. and by the way Bill Wahl has just got his too. Brother Bill is on Ferry Command[xxi] and hopes to be over here in the near future. He and I will sure have a party the day he arrives. I have been looking forward to that day for a long time.

Had a very quiet Xmas and New Years but received a lot of nice mail from friends back home which helped to make up for what was missing.

Believe it or not I still prefer the Can. Girls even after meeting some very swell ones from Eng., Scot and Wales. Have considered getting married several times over here but so far I haven't been able to settle down enough to make up my mind.

Don't think that I will either while I am flying.

Please give my best to all your family Bill and wish them a Happy New Year for me.

Let's hope that I won't be quite so far away from Vanc. by this time next year.

Bye for now and all the best Cpl.

> Your friend
>
> Earl

S.D. Treadgold
Kelowna, B.C.

Jan.19th 1943

Dear Bill-

Received your letter written at Jim's, tonight. Glad you are fine. Well, we have had some terrible weather since I wrote you around 10 below or better. It is still cold but not so bad. Quite stormy with snow blowing all over. It is best to be in the house where I keep it warm. It was so cold yesterday I kept Barry home. He had a cold anyway and the rest seemed to do him good. He sat playing with his building set and doing cross words or rather jigsaw puzzles. He is surely very good at putting them together and will sit a long time working it out. Oh, how I hate this cold weather. I sent you the cookies so hope they won't be frozen. We have had nothing like this for years. I keep thinking of the poor Russians but I expect they are more used to it than we are. Barry says they are dressed for it. I hear that sawdust will be rationed before long, even here. The whole country is surely in one mess but I hope we see it through.

Ann Curts has been drafted to Halifax. Frances will miss her so. She is still in Galt but does not know when and where she will go, she says one never knows. Frances expects to spend this weekend with the girls in Toronto.

This Thursday is the church supper but I don't know who will be going as some today will have to stay in to look after fires and Barry. Donna has not been going to school for over a week but she went to-day. It has been dark and she had a cold too. They have been learning in the dark. They went with Dad about 8:30 but to-day it was a quarter to nine and it seemed a little lighter. Barry walked home in the cold and was fine. They are both asked to Fumertons to a party on Friday. Turner still hits up the Legion. Dad says the shop is nice and warm. Everybody that comes in says how warm it is. Dad says they earned it after being frozen for 20 years or more. I hear that Dr. Knox has Toxic Goitre so that may be right and he may get well again.

Well Bill I will have to try and make a different kind of cookie for a change although we use quite a lot of oatmeal cookies. Sugar and fruit also nuts are hard to get so one can only use so much but I will make something before those run out. I have not seen much of Miles lately - too cold. He went with Jack over to the Frances' to skate and had a hockey stick, he told Barry he was playing hockey. It was so cold he was only there a few minutes but I believe the skating will be fine there. Miles is very much like his dad used to be, quite a bluffer. He phoned me the other day and told me to get started making paste as his was all gone and he wanted some more. The kids are all pretty good on the phone now. I have not much news. We are all as usual. I hope you don't have to go overseas, but if you do, we will have to make the best of it but I surely wouldn't ask for it.

They say there is a thin skin over the lake. Let's hope this does not keep up or it will surely freeze over. Somebody on the ferry was saying that they did not know how this ferry would make it. Some of the new comers think this some winter. However, we old timers think it better than the winters gone by.

Well Bill I will add more tomorrow so bye for now.

      With heaps of love from us all

        Mother

Well Bill I got my letter off to Annemarie so that's done, and by the way Toby jugs are jugs with faces, very often small - get them in jewelry stores or china shops. They are quite expensive, quite nice, sometimes used as match holders etc. Quite a nice gift to keep.

The weather is fierce to-day cold and blustery.

I will have to get lunch

So be good.

Hope you're fine

Mother

B. Arthur
2171 St. Luke St.
Apt. 8 – Montreal

Thur. Feb 11/43.

Dear Bill

How are things going? It's been a long time since you last saw this hand-writing eh?

Afraid my correspondence has gone to the dogs lately, but now that I'm pretty well confined to the house with a bad cold I'm trying to write a few overdue letters. I managed to get a few addresses from Head Office and having written Russ Scrim I must say "Hello" to you. How do you like Pat Bay Bill? I was out there several times when they were completing that station, but I guess it has changed a lot since then.

I hear you have been having some pretty bad weather lately. Over here had a real tough winter and to really make things nice it decided to rain so you can imagine condition the streets are in, which causes a bit of tie-up in transportation.

I'm rather fortunate in being centrally located - about 15 min walk from the office, and 20 min from the centre of the city. We are really working hard these days Bill - as you can well imagine at Victoria Ave. - where we once had 12 men and 4 girls we now have 4 men and 13 girls. They're a pretty good bunch though. We manage to get the work through and keep the office in shape with a little night work. They are sure closing a lot of branches here, however, we are fortunate in being so situated that we are not likely to have another branch to take over.

I trust you are dealing with Douglas St. branch in Vict. And if so give my regards to Miss Pearson next time you are in - I believe Mr. Ross, the mgr. has been seriously ill.

Is the Kong still out of bounds for you boys? We had the Chinese business at Douglas St and so I know most of the "big shots" from China-Town - they were really a swell bunch though and used to treat us royally.

This is quite a city Bill and I'm hoping you'll be passing through some day and have a few hours to spare - what will it be - blonde? - I thought so -

Well W.O. hope this finds you well and not being over-worked.

Say, is MacDougall still at Kelowna? Did we love him eh?

    So long for now Bill

       Bill Arthur

S.D. Treadgold

Kelowna, B.C.

Feb 15th 1943.

Dear Bill-

It is time I was dropping you a line. You will be wondering where I am. We are still here and Wilma is some better again. Some friends of hers have been taking her out and giving it a trial to see if they can help her so I hope it continues. They had a game of table tennis to-night and went to a friend's home. Yesterday she was out with a bunch, tomorrow night she is going again so it is good of them to come and take her in the car etc. If this does not help, she will have to have more shocks[xxii]. She has never said anything crazy since we were in Vancouver but she may be thinking it. I don't know. She is eating well and looks in better health so perhaps some day it will clear away. It will have to for I could not stand it. The weather is nice with lots of slush snow and water. Mr. McLeod is in hospital. Dad went to see him tonight. I will give you Frances latest address

L/W Treadgold. FM. WRENS. S-89 Rideau St., Ottawa

She says the room she works in is the nicest one in the building and she is in it most of the time from morning until mid night. She was hoping they would give her another regulator. She seems quite happy. They had just given her the afternoon off and she had a million jobs to do. I will have to get busy with the cookies again - try and get them off this week.

Barry reads very well now. It is nice to hear him. He and Miles are quite interested in games and puzzles and they do very well. These kids will soon all be grown up. Dad is busy framing new pictures and he has made a bunch of nice trays. I am going to send one to Jim. I must drop Jim a line. I had a nice letter from him on Saturday. I scalded my wrist not badly but I can see some blood I got on this page so excuse - I rubbed most of it off. I have not sent the Courier yet but will tomorrow.

Tuesday morning-

10 A.M.

Well Bill I don't seem to have any more news but we are all fine and it is quite mild. I will now get at my cooking and see what I can do so drop a line when you have time and I will write soon.

    With lots of love

       Mother

               Enclosed letter from Frances dated Feb. 1

Dear Mother-

Here I am in Ottawa - drafted at last. I received notice about three o'clock Wednesday, left Thursday at noon and arrived here late Thursday night.

We are opening up a barracks for Wrens here very soon and I am here to help get things going. At present I am living at Hardy House, eating at Kingsmill House and working at the Seminarium which is the building which has been taken over for the Wrens. It is a very old place and needs a lot of fixing over - I am very anxious to see just what they'll make of it.

Your last letter was forwarded from Galt and I received it at noon. Also had one from Anne who is in bed with a cold. She says very little about Halifax.

As yet I've had no time at all to look around. Went to town Saturday morning and bought myself some new shoes - the issue ones were just about killing me. My feet are still tender but I'm hoping the new shoes will straighten me out.

Saturday night nineteen of us went over to Hull Quebec to have dinner at Madame Burger's. We had a wonderful meal - the whole evening was spent in dining. It was really worth the $2 we had to pay.

It isn't very cold here but there is plenty of snow - it is piled high on the sides of the streets.

Marion Miles who is married to Capt. Pennington lives just around the corner from here. At present she is visiting in Cranbrook while her husband is in England.

I'll write again in a day or two. Everything is so new and jumbled up that it is hard to get things sorted out or to know what to say.

Hope you are all well and not too cold.

Love,

Frances

STANDARD ONE-EGG COOKIES
Sugar Cookies

½ cup butter or other shortening	1½ cups Five Roses Flour
½ cup sugar	1½ teaspoons baking powder
1 beaten egg-yolk	⅛ teaspoon salt
3 tablespoons milk	½ teaspoon vanilla

Mix as directed; make rolled or ice box cookies. Bake as directed.

BUTTERSCOTCH COOKIES

1 cup butter	½ teaspoon salt
2 cups light brown sugar	1 teaspoon baking soda
2 eggs, unbeaten	½ teaspoon baking powder
3½ cups Five Roses Flour	1 teaspoon vanilla

NOTE.—When eggs are expensive, use only one, and add 2 tablespoons of milk.

Sift soda with flour, baking powder and salt. Then mix as directed. Chill the mixture VERY thoroughly, as the dough is soft and is difficult to handle if it is not cold. Make rolled or ice-box cookies, rolling or cutting the dough very thin. Place on greased baking sheet, decorate as desired, and bake in a moderately hot oven, 375 to 400 deg. F.

For a cookie that is less sweet, use 1½ cups brown sugar.

Delicious cookies for special occasions are made by adding ½ cup each of glace cherries, walnut meats and raisins, and ¼ cup each of cut citron and candied ginger, all put through the mincer. Mix well with the dough, mould, wrap, chill, cut and bake as directed.

S.D. Treadgold's cookie recipes

S.D. Treadgold

Kelowna, B.C.

Feb 23rd 43 Tuesday

Dear Bill-

Your letter received to-day and I am a little late getting mine off. We are all fine and I had a nice letter from Frances to-day she is working hard but is getting an experienced regulator to help her and she has been getting some time off.

I had a letter from Auntie Annie in Kitchener and she asked me to tell you to write as they liked to hear from you. She seems to be worrying over the boys having to go in the Army. She says she has no big laughs left, which is too bad and that Millie in Toronto was not too well. Barry had a birthday yesterday and I made him a nice cake and Dad brought home a pair of breeks [pants] with pockets and does he like them. He is 7. He wants a bike with a bar. So he is quite the boy. He can read so well.

Well I have to get those cookies off yet. I had the paper hangers here and have the living room and hall done over so I had that to straighten etc. but will send them very soon.

Wilma is not as good as we would like to see her. Dr. Henderson said that was the unfortunate part they get these set backs. So we might take her down yet. She is out this afternoon visiting a girl friend. If I go to Vancouver I will write Jim and let you know.

Mr. McLeod has gone home from hospital. He had a cold and was quite sick but is much better. Our snow has almost gone but the last two nights have been cold, the days like spring. Bob was up last night we have not seen very much of him. He was skating when it was on and Jones is in Vancouver delivering the boat they built. Mazie was over on Thursday night and we enjoyed her visit. I hear there is a boy in C.K.O.V. that looks so much like you that he has been asked several times if he is Bill Treadgold. Rev. McPherson was telling Dad.

I have not nearly so much work on the board now Mr. Bryden has taken over a lot of it. I will send the paper on. Hunts store is now a large ration office.

I am glad you are in the quarter you like best. It is nice to be comfortable. Dad has just put Barry to bed. He is very good to go to sleep now.

I hope spring is just around the corner and I expect all will as the 'fireing' has been quite a task. I should go and make a batch of cookies and cook them in the morning perhaps I will after I read the paper. The nights seem longer with this daylight saving. Dad comes home at 5 o'clock.

I will add more tomorrow is I can think but will close now with my love

     Mother

Started on the eats to-day Bill.

F.J. Henderson

Chilliwack

March 30th 1943

Dear Bill,

I have a daughter living in Victoria, "Mrs. H.G. France" 18 Wellington Ave. I have mentioned your name in writing to her saying you are a "Kelowna" boy, friend of Ben O'Shaw and mine also. Kathleen, Mrs. Fraser would be very pleased to have you come out to her home when you are in Victoria. You could call her up, she is a few blocks from the town, easy place to find. Kathleen has her married daughter living with her. Mr. and Mrs. Gilbul-Yard have two children. Mr. Yard lives by school out at "Oak Bay".

John Fraser, my grandson, is in the R.C.A.F. at MacDonald Manitoba. I am taking it for granted you are still at Patricia Bay. Geo Webb and his wife were visiting Chilliwack a short time ago with the second Webb boy Josh, and Earl last week. I understand he will be in the Airforce too. We are having such a lot of rain now and quite cold too; snow way down on the mountains. It certainly is a late spring everyone is anxious to get busy with their gardens, especially vegetables this year.

I often see Mr. Brown, poor old fellow he looks frail, and his eyesight is getting worse, I think, but he is always cheerful and asking after everyone. I enjoyed your nice long letter – pleased the socks were right size. Have not heard from Stan for a few weeks, but I dare say he is very busy.

You know Dr. Knox has been ill and away down to "Mayos" for an operation. I understand he is home, but it will be sometime before the Dr will be able to practice. Did you know the Russels in Kelowna? I think Mr. Paul Russel had something to do with the Kelowna Hospital, well we have Mr. Paul Russel in Chilliwack now, he is manager of our Hospital. The family came early last fall. I like the Russels very much. Our Hospital Aux is getting ready for a big dance on the 3rd of April - is to be a big affair. (one expects to make some money).

I am in the Royal Bank quite often, must go this week again. In both banks so many new girls. I suppose it is the same everywhere. Now I must close. Hope this finds you quite well and that you will enjoy your visit to my daughters.

Sincerely yours

Frances J. Henderson

"Keep in touch with the folks at home"

ON ACTIVE SERVICE

WITH THE

CANADIAN FORCES

20 April 1943

K-20 L/Cpl. Krasselt A.W.
H.Q. Sqn. 9th Arm'd Regt. (B.C.D.)
Cdn. Army Overseas

April 20/43

Dear Oscar

Yes kid it's just about time I got around to dropping you a line however you did beat me to it with
your dated 8 Mar received a few days ago. Honestly
though Bill I've been so G.D. busy that I was
even two months late going on leave. No, I'm not
beefing but I really hate to let my letter writing
get so far behind, however all is fair in love and
war, and at present at least I'm not getting much
of the former. But don't get me wrong. I do step
out every chance I get to see my Viennese friend.
However will forget about that for the moment and
get down to brass tacks.

Was certainly very pleased to receive your letter
Bill and hear about Russ Scrim, Eldith etc. How are
they all doing? God how I would like to see them
all again — and you too you old so and so. Please
remember me to all Bill, and give 'em my best.

As I said before Bill my leave was 2 months late,
however I did get it and returned just a week ago

today. As per usual I had a very nice time, however I still am not very thrilled with London — It's too damn big especially now that transportation quits so early. If you stay some distance from the West End and therefore require transportation "home" one has to get going about 11 o'clock and you know me — that's just too early. However, it was all very enjoyable.

Joyce Chapman and I arranged to have a couple of days together and really enjoyed ourselves very much. We saw two very good plays, the film "Commando Strike at Dawn", went dancing and visited and toured all through the Tower of London. The plays we saw were the "Merry Widow" which was extremely good and "The Man Who Came to Dinner". The former of course was a musical comedy and for that reason I enjoyed it much more than the later (drama). However they were both very well acted. The Tower of London was very interesting and brought back memories of the old History Periods in school — not so pleasant.

The rest of my leave was spent entertaining Cousins and we carried on much as usual seeing films and shows, dancing, sight seeing and most of all eating very well (for this country). Had lots of dough this time but God those pound notes don't seem to go as far as the old dollar bill used to. I peeled off 22 of them in nine days, and at that my board and room was five, so you can see that it takes the dough to go on leave in this country.

Another interesting thing I did was to go all through the Daily Sketch Newspaper plant. As the Vanc Province did when we (The Choir Boys) were in

Vanc they made up our names in lead as a souvenir. 'Nough about that.

The weather here is just perfect. You'd really think that it was the good old summer time. Especially with the double daylight saving. It soon will be daylight 'till midnight. No fun walking your baby back home these days. 'Course I wouldn't know, but that's what the boys keep telling me.

Attended our weekly dance last Friday, but didn't enjoy it as much as usual. Yes, she was there, but my "gut" has been giving me hell lately and I just wasn't feeling any too good. I therefore did very little dancing, but hope to do better this week.

Was out canoeing on Sunday on a small river — wish it had been good old Okanagan Lake — or Beaver Lake, but it was O.K. just the same. Rounded off the day by going out for supper, and then running like hell to catch the last bus back to camp. God what a life. I've nearly had to walk that 10 miles several times — guess I'll have to pick a gal closer to "home" in future — or sumpin. She's really nice though Bill — but don't get any ideas 'cause I suppose when we pull stakes again she'll just be another in the passing parade.

Well kid it's nearly midnight and as you can see by my scribble I'm ready to sign off and hit the hay.

Write again soon Bill — and in the meantime do as I do and keep it in your own drawers.

Hoping that this finds you well and "happy in the soivice".

This is "Best of Luck" Oscar.

As ever

    Your Pal

        Krass

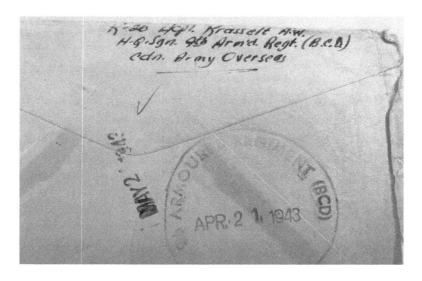

K-20 L/Cpl. Krasselt A.W.

H.Q. Sqn. 9th Arm'd Regt. (B.C.D.)

Cdn. Army Overseas

10 May 43 (typed letter)

Dear Bill:-

Thanks a lot Bill for you "Airgraph" received a couple of days ago. Sure swell to hear from you Kid, and know that you are able to spend a leave at home. God how I've forgotten what that is like, but manage to have a lot of fun spending them at someone else's home. Often think though of how nice it would be to come home from work, and with nothing else to do, say: well I guess I'll wander down to the Acquatic and see what's doing. God there I go spelling aquatic wrong, but as you know me, I'll let it go.

It's sure hard to write letters these days Oscar 'cause except for the fact that I step out on Wednesday and Saturday nights when I can, and of course nearly every Sunday, my social life is sadly neglected, and that is what seems to make the news. Even on those days it's the same old routine, as the town we go to is quite small. On Wed night it is usually the pictures, Sat night a dance, and on Sunday a walk in the afternoon, and then to the girl friend's place for supper. Believe it or not it is the same girl friend too, but that part is far from boring.

As maybe I told you before, I am scabbing on the job now, and holding down two of them at once. I was busy before, but now that I do quite a bit of driving as well, I find that even my nights are taken up into the wee small hours of the morning.

Last week it was really hectic, but as I'm off tonight, it looks as though this week is off to a better start.

That fishing you speak of really sounds interesting, bet it was a real thrill to land that nine pounder.

Is it ever a dirty night out tonight. Looks as though we are getting the March winds and April showers, all together, and you can imagine how nice that is. However we can't kick as the former months were really grand.

Glad to hear that Eldith, Phillipa, and the Chapmans are all keeping well, wrote a line to Mr. & Mrs. last week, but as Eldith, Eric, Hap, etc., all owe me letter, and due to the fact that I just haven't got the time to carry on with the load of correspondence that I used to, I'm patiently awaiting a reply from them.

I know that this is very short Bill, but there just isn't another word to say. Will therefore just have to say, "Au revoir" and hope to hear from you again soon. Until then this is as ever, loadsa good luck to you Kid, and write again soon.

Your pal

Krass

S.D. Treadgold
Kelowna, B.C.

June 23 / 43.

Dear Bill-

Well Bill I know you will wonder, what or why I have not written. We are all fine but I have been so busy. Things have moved fast lately. Harold has rented the house for Dad, really, but without fuss of any kind, it is almost like a fairy tale. I think he is going to Vancouver for the summer months. Anyway, Dad and I had all the work to do getting the stuff out and stored etc. and when night came I was not up to writing a decent letter.

Frances was here for a couple of days when we knew first and Barry was down with the mumps. It was a fairly mild case and he is fine. Will be off to school tomorrow I think Miles is in bed today and I would not be surprised if later on Donna has them too. It's good to get it over with. The other people are in the house.

Dad asked Harold where he was going to stay, and he said there on the Veranda but Dad thought they did not want to have him around so told him to come and sleep on our Veranda, thinking he was going to Vancouver in a few days. Yesterday he said he was not going until some time next month. So, I have

Barry and Donna with Dad Harold

the whole works. He is in Summerland two days will be back tonight.

The kiddies are dandy with me but when he is around it is anything but quiet, so I am afraid Dad will be saying something before a month. He does not come for lunch except on Sunday.

I have said nothing to Wilma, as it is hard to put in a letter so for the time, I have not mentioned the house. I wrote her this morning too. Harold told her awhile ago he might be going to Vancouver for the summer months, stored the furniture etc. in Sutherlands Furniture Store and the small stuff I have here to look after and put in shape in time. Everything is fine so she does not need to worry. I got a letter from Frances and she is just back and had a letter saying she had to give her "famous" speech Thursday morning. It always makes her shiver. She will get used to it. This is a scribble but I must get it off. I wrote Jim as he too will think me terrible. I think perhaps now we will have more time with only one house to look after.

Well Bill don't worry over your work as you know it does not pay, but one always has to stand on their own feet and stick up for yourself.

I will have to drop Frances a line. We got the watch and took it in to Pettigrews last Saturday and thanks for sending Dad the card and writing me the letters. Don't think I forget or really get careless for I don't, but from now on I hope to have more time to myself.

I want to put this in the mail so excuse. With my love. I promise to write soon again

As ever

    Your Mother

      Don Treadgold

If you see Wilma let me know Bill please.

S.D. Treadgold
Kelowna, B.C.

July 4th / 43

Dear Bill

Well, I have just written Frances a line so will drop you one too. I am pleased you went to see Wilma. I have not heard from her. She told Frances she had nothing to write about so that may be true too but Frances told her to write anyway. I wish she would hurry and get well. It's such a slow business.

The weather is lovely these days, we sat on the beach to-day it was not too warm. Barry, Donna and Miles are going to Lake swimming lessons at the aquatic starting tomorrow.

Well sent you a few cookies yesterday. I got a hustle on in the morning and Dad said the box was warm when mailed. He also sent your watch.

Well you had quite a time on your last 48. Dad had quite a laugh with you having 25¢ in your pocket. Not much danger of being held up and robbed of a large sum. Frances is fine and has seven girls under her now in the office.

Barry was sick for a couple of days but is better again. Jack is quite busy with the aquatic. I think there is quite a good membership.

I heard yesterday that Philip Russell was missing but it may not be right, also Harry Lyon who was in the Bank of Montreal was believed killed.

I went up town last night and such a lot of strangers. The town is full of them. I didn't know anybody. You can't rent a house in town they say. Mr. Stubbs and Harry Campbell are both going to Military camp in Vernon tomorrow for 2 weeks. We still have a few teachers to get. It is quite a job now. It is just 10 o'clock and I must drop a line to Wilma although I have little news.

Write when you can and I hope you are well.

    With my love

        Mother

Monday morn.

We are fine and the kids had their first lesson this morning.

Hope you have received the cookies.

    With my love

        Mother

S.D. Treadgold

Kelowna, B.C.

July 14th / 43

Dear Bill

All your letters received and very welcome Bill also glad you are feeling better. We are all fine. I should have written last night but went up to Marge's for a little while. It is just 2 o'clock and if I get these letters written will go to mail this afternoon. Glad to hear you think Wilma better she has not written, she may have little to write about. I expect she got the sweater etc. that I sent. I am pleased that Jean would be seeing her.

The weather is very nice but showery to-day, however we need the rain.

Congratulations on receiving your stripes. It is nice to know where you stand.

The children are fine and Barry can do the shopping now he gets me milk and bread etc. He is quite proud of himself, goes on his bike with the basket, he thinks himself quite the shopper.

Both he and Miles can swim a little. They go for lessons. Donna goes tomorrow. They had so many it is just once a week now, until they can swim well and then twice.

Dad made them a nice sort of surf board and paddle and they have a good time, take it down on their wagon to the lake here. He painted it sun flower yellow and black, just a little black. It is for the three of them. All have their initials on it. Miles wanted one for each. Miles would like a small boat.

I will send you cookies this week I think I have some made.

I see by the paper Phillip is missing.

I must write Frances she was in bed for a day the same time as you with a sore ingrown toe nail. The Dr. fixed it so hope she is better again. And Jim, I must drop him a line, I had a nice letter from him and hope to see them before long. I have a board meeting tonight so thought I would get a line off now, hope you are fine and your letters are always welcome, so many thanks

       With my love

         Mother

"Keep in touch with the folks at home"

ON ACTIVE SERVICE
WITH THE
CANADIAN FORCES

          K-20 L/Cpl. Krasselt A.W.
     H.Q. Sqn. 9th Arm'd Regt. (B.C.D.)
             Cdn. Army Overseas

               14 July 43

Dear Bill:-

Please excuse me typing this Bill, and also my typing, but my pen has gone haywire, so have had to resort to this.

First of all I'd like to thank you very much for the swell letter that I received a couple of days ago. It was dated June 10 so took just about a month to cross. What a letter --- just imagine 12 pages. Sorry Bill but I just can't compete with that. All the news I have could be written on the back of a postage stamp in block letters, however I'll see what I can do about filling up a page or two.

That C.P.R. note paper certainly brings back fond memories of the days when we were in Victoria, and had the pleasure of spending time the odd weekend in Vancouver. What a time we used to have when crossing, with Don Bickerton on the piano and everyone half shot trying to sing. Those were the days.

We are now situated right out in God's country, but unlike the show, there is no Women. However a change is as good as a rest --- so we'll just make the best of it. It's really swell to be out in the country again though, and will give us a chance to save a little "dough" for another leave -- if we get one.

Yes, Bill one has no trouble finding a lady friend over here, 'cause as you know they have a big majority over the men in this country, and after you have taken them out a couple of times the situation becomes very serious as they all seem to be husband hunting. What a life. Really have a swell little gal near our old camp. She is from Vienna, and is really a "cute dish". She is very different from the English Girls in fact very like the good old Canadians. She has only been in this country for four years, but speaks English so perfectly that had she not told me that she was foreign I'd never have known it. Really hated to leave our other joint for that reason, but after-all we're in the Army now. By the way how are you making out with your young Lady in Lethbridge? Haven't heard you mention her for ages. Come on -- give.

Certainly was tough about Harry Lawson, also his Mother. God when one thinks what a war does to people, it really gets you down.

Well Bill this seems to be all for this time, I know that it is very short, but there just isn't any news.

Will therefore say au revoir, and don't forget Kid, if you ever land over here for God sake give me your address or sumpin as soon as possible after your arrival, and we'll get together on a damn good tear of some kind.

Hoping to hear from you soon, and next time I'll try to scare up a more interesting sort of letter. Until then this is, as ever

Your pal

    Krass

S.D. Treadgold
Kelowna, B.C.
July 19th / 43

Dear Bill -

Well Bill here it is Monday and quite a warm day.
I am writing this on the front veranda where it is
quite nice.

I had a letter from Wilma and she would like to
come back home while the treatments are stopped.
The doctor and some of the nurses are having a
3-week holiday - but it means we would have to
go get her. Some of them do go home for weekends
etc. but this is quite a way and it is difficult
with the children. I feel sorry to disappoint her.
Harold is still here and we have not heard another
word about the transfer. I am wondering just what
is brewing. I sent Wilma a couple of new dresses
which I hope will fit her. We are having real
summer weather to-day. Dad went for a swim yesterday so it must be hot.

I sent you the paper but have not sent the cookies
yet. I keep busy, three extra for meals makes
quite a lot all the time. I don't get much time to
do a lot - I would like to have Wilma's things all
washed up and put away nicely. It is a good thing
she has a mother to look after her stuff. I am
afraid she would not have had much as everything
was surely let go. I am wondering if Jim and Vie
will be coming this way. I am glad Betty had a nice
wedding and I hope they are well.

We have not heard from Frances just lately but
expect she is fine. They say that most of the

soldiers have left Vernon. I expect they are shifting them on. Quite a number come to Kelowna for the weekend. I expect it is nice for a change, I would like to go someplace myself some times, everybody needs some come and go.

Frances finds the weather very hot and sticky. It will be better with her summer uniform. When she had her toenail fixed the knife slipped and the doctor had to put a stitch in but she never knew until she removed the bandage.

Freddie Thompson has been in town for a couple of days with Jack. The kids were quite excited over the sailor uniform.

Barry was out in the boat yesterday and can now row, he looks to me to be a born rower, but I don't think he should do it. He was so tired this morning I had to feed him his breakfast.

Barry rowing the Hi Ho with Uncle Jim Palframan

Peter Murdock is out of the army (health). The girls seem to be joining up and going one by one but we seem to have such a lot of strangers or new people. Dad's man MacCormak may be leaving going East perhaps. We have been asked to rent the cottage enough already and it is not certain, news travels fast. They say you can't get a house.

I see Mr. Pettigrew is in town. I don't know how long for.

Miles is as tough as ever. He is so strong, the surfboard Dad made them is good to make them active in the water. Miles says his dad owns the Aquatic.

I must drop a line to Frances. I will have to go visiting and get some news. You can't get it staying at home. When Frances was here I got all the local news. I sometimes wish I could ride a bicycle, to see the numbers go by here.

My garden is quite nice now bright with quite a lot of colour more than usual. It may be the cooler weather brought them on better. We have had quite a bit of wind, not very severe, but you can hear the lake.

So you think Kelowna kids O.K. I do too on the whole. I think perhaps they will be able to hold their own anywhere.

We have a grand new bridge over the creek by Haug's, both traffic and foot bridge and a grand new road and side walk. They are making a good job of roads etc. now. They are improving the park and aquatic and have put a lot of work there this year by what they say, a lot of property has changed hands so people must be coming in.

Well I will write to Frances now. And thanks for the letters. I will send the eats soon.

So with my love

Mother

The Kelowna Aquatic, Ribelin photo

S.D. Treadgold

Kelowna, B.C.

Aug 1st / 43

Dear Bill –

You will wonder what has happened to me again, well nothing just busy as usual. I have been doing fruit and quite a lot of it – cherries, raspberries, black currents and apricots – all at once it seems fruit is very hard to get. Harold's got some down the lake and some I got privately. It's very expensive this year so far. So I will have some jam when you come home. The weather is very warm but nice. The children are in the lake almost every afternoon and they can swim and are getting to be water rats, in fact I go in most days myself so that is pretty good for me I enjoy it very much but I do keep busy, I have quite a family now you know. It seems no let up.

The Regatta will be on this week, everybody seems busy. You will be surprised and sorry to hear two soldier boys were drowned on Thursday night just this side of the Aquatic -, dangerous place. Jack saw them a few minutes before but no body missed them for hours, it was just after six o'clock when most people were gone. They think they could not swim. I expect one went to help the other. They were working on a barge for the soldiers. They were told not to go there to swim but I guess they thought it alright. They got one body Friday and one to-day. I believe very few know of it and a good thing as it would sort of put a gloom over the regatta.

Jack had jumped and asked 'what was that noise?' and Audrey Hughes told him it was the kids down below, but now he thinks it may have been one calling. He was quite cut up about it and helped all day Friday. He saw the army shirt there at nine o'clock but thought one of the soldiers working had left it. Two boys from the Prairie, one was an instructor – about 25 years old. They will have to fence that part in as that is where all accidents seem to happen.

There is a big sign there.

I have not heard from Wilma or Frances lately. I had a letter from Violet and she seemed to think Wilma some better, did you get out? Will be glad when it's time to take her out if that ever comes.

Barry lost one of his top teeth to-day eating an apple, so that is the third one to go, two at the bottom, he looks funny.

I have not sent the paper yet as Dad had not read it.

The kids are surely having a good time this summer. They row the boat and give the kids a ride and dive off the boat. We watch them all the time. This is perfect weather for the lake.

Alison and Miles were up for supper so there were 7 of us. I seem to have 5 or 6 all the time and they get hungry too. We did not get our paper to-day but I heard the Sun papers were in. We have rented the cottage where Jim was, again to Dick Jacobson in McKenzie. He sold his place. We had so many people after it, homes are so very scarce, you can't get anything. MacCormak went East. We seem to have good tenants in our houses, a good thing too.

I must do you some cookies at once. I intended to send some last week but the fruit kept me too busy and these kids are quite a handful and we have a lot of new teachers to get again, that is all done or nearly so for another year. I often wonder how people do war work as I have all I can do without it. I guess I am not so fast as I used to be, but I can do enough yet. Everybody is in bed so I will go too and don't worry if my letter is a day late. I keep thinking of you and the others away. I like writing often but some times it gets put off and then a day or so has gone. I will write Violet and Frances tomorrow.

Hope to hear from you soon again. So, I will say goodnight for now.

    With my love,

        Mother

                S.D. Treadgold
                Kelowna, B.C.

                Aug. 18th / 43

Dear Bill-

Your letter received Bill and as usual they are welcome. Glad you are getting around. We are all fine and the weather has been grand. It would have been nice to have had you for the Regatta. I must send in the last paper. The Regatta was quite a success.

We have still not heard a word of Wilma or from her. So, if you can make time go and see what and how things are. I hope Dad or one of us here will be able to go down. I want Dad to. I think a change would be good for his nerves as he seems to have been tired lately between one thing and another. Wilma could at least drop a line but it seems she won't, so what that means, I wonder. If she is not so well, I would just as soon know it as wonder. I don't worry I have too much to do.

Anna Marie Fumerton's cousin is here, she spent a month with them in Lethbridge and came to speak to me. Anna sent her regards.

Mr. Fumerton left for Lethbridge for a holiday. I don't know whether Mrs. went or not but I don't think so.

Barry went to the shop for awhile, he likes it there. Donna is playing with Miles, they get on quite well.

Bruce P. phoned. Dad answered the phone so I did not talk to him.

Jack has a place, for your friend, at the May Fair which is the best and they can use the Aquatic so that should be alright.

The town is so full of strangers that there is not anybody that knows many people. One wonders where they came from.

Barry, Donna and Miles at Vimy Beach in Kelowna

It is just 10:30. The time goes quickly. Dad has a couple of extra men but they are not very good and he sometimes gets fed up with them. He turns down much more work than he does, but it can't be helped.

I will be glad when school starts. The kids are pretty good and have had a good summer and surely love the water and they are veterans at rowing. They handle the oars well. Dad wonders how they do it - swim and jump in.

We expect a large load of box ends. The only one we will get as it is scarce this year and I am going to have my hair done this afternoon so I am full up to-day.

I have very little news for you but I will send the paper to-day. Try and see Wilma and let us know.

Hope you are fine and write soon.

    With my love

        Mother

                    S.D. Treadgold
                    Kelowna, B.C.

                    Aug. 25th / 43

Dear Bill -

Well Bill thanks for the letter and going to see Wilma, also for the box of candy.

Both Dad and I feel very badly about Wilma, it does seem to take so long and we can only hope. I was rather expecting to hear she was not so good, as I can tell how she goes, but I do hope in the end she will get better. It does seem too bad; she can be so nice and the children need her. I think Dad is going to have a talk with Harold very soon and see what his plans are, as we really don't want him and I don't think it is up to us to have to change our plans and live as we like. He never says a word about anything.

I am writing this at the beach with the two children. They wanted to come down and it is simply grand. I feel badly that Wilma has to live where she is - how terrible it all is, however in time I will do something if she does not improve.

I heard yesterday that Dan Lucas was killed in Sicily but I am not certain.

Dad is feeling better, he is taking lemon and tomato juice in the morning, somebody recommended it to him.

I had a letter from Frances and she is fine, busy as usual.

Last Friday I had a surprise - Maudie Kincaid spent the day in Kelowna and called on me. I was so pleased to see her, she is fine and works up at the Sanatorium, something like a teacher, looks after the correspondence courses for those that like it. She seemed very happy and she has been through a lot.

When you go to see Wilma you have just to pay 50¢ I think when you're in uniform - so Frances said. She reminded them and that is all she paid so let me know and I will send you to cover the expense. When will anybody see her again? I only hope and pray that she will get better.

Barry and Donna surely enjoy the water. They are so changed along that line, when they come out they lie on their towels and enjoy it so.

There are a lot of people here to-day. The weather is grand.

Many thanks for the candy Bill. School is the next thing on the programme. We have had quite a lot of people here from Vancouver this summer in fact a great number of them - they came to the beach here too.

Well Bill I have little news for you but I wanted to let you know I appreciate you going to see Wilma, it may help her. I only wish I could go sometimes.

So with my love and many thanks

As ever

Your Mother

S.D. Treadgold
Kelowna, B.C.

Sept 2nd / 43

Dear Bill -

Well here it is Thursday again and I thought I would get a line off to you as Dad may be going to Vancouver for the weekend to see Wilma. I expect he will leave to-morrow night (Friday) and go to have a talk with Wilma also the doctors. It is only right that we should go and see how she is. Your last report was not very good and I don't expect anybody has been since as we have heard nothing and we didn't expect Violet to go as she not may want to. It is rather a strain on us not to know. We understand quite a bit and are not blind to the case but even so we want to do what we can for her. I expect Jim is busy but he could drop a line as he has only written twice since the first of April and I think I had letters from Violet anyway. Dad is going down and I expect to go down and to Victoria about the 25th Sept. If you did not go once in a while, we would hear very little. I have been looking for a line from Wilma but not yet so I expect she is not much better.

Harold is not with us now. Dad told him he had better get accom up town, so he got one and we are alone with the children and I think it is better for all concerned. It was too hard on Dad's nerves.

The weather is a little colder. It was so windy for 3 days and still is a little.

If you get over to see Dad he will give you all the news but there is not a lot to write about.

I expect to hear from Frances soon. I heard she might be getting a commission but she never said anything about it.

It's just eleven o'clock so I will get busy with lunch. If I should get a letter today I will add a line. We have had lunch but still no news so I guess this is all. I must get busy and make cookies again so you will get some one of these days.

Thanks for the letter Bill. They are always so welcome and I hope to see you before too long so bye

      with my love

         Mother

                  S.D. Treadgold
                  Kelowna, B.C.

                  Sept 10th / 43

Dear Bill-

Well Bill I hope you have recovered from your disappointment and are fine again. It is too bad you missed Dad. He too was disappointed but he kept busy going to see Wilma. It is quite a trip there. Dad got back to-day. I wish he could have had more of a holiday as he does not look too good. He said Wilma seemed some better and they had some talk, however the treatments started on Wednesday and he saw her in the afternoon and she was better. He has promised to get her when the treatments end so she is looking forward to that but it is up to her so she should try. Jim did not think her very good one day but Dad says she has been so much worse. She was quiet. He was out 4 times. The doctor said she was not so good but it was because of the long time without treatment, short of nurses and doctors. Dad says he can see where they didn't get the care etc. that wouldn't be good for them. Simply short of help.

Dad told her she would have to break from Harold and forget the past etc. both go their own way. I can't see anything else for it at the present. It will take a time to get things going again. But she will take a job when the time comes. Dad says when she comes out she can stay at Ludlows or Bert's as well be alone. Joan leaves for Calgary next Monday and Barbara is at Feedhams' most of the time. So perhaps things will work their way out.

The children are at DeHart and fine. The Ludlows gave Wilma a nice pup, a Blue Kerry. 7 weeks old. We have it here - a little beauty and the kids love it. They promised Wilma one some two or more years ago so we will have to take good care of it. I should have written you sooner but really, I get so tired lately with doing fruit, jam, pickles etc. and I feel I must do them this year, and the kids. I had two board meetings this week, however I have a lot of fruit so that is nice and will be nice for winter. I hope to leave here on the 24th, see Wilma on Saturday then go to Victoria Sunday morning and stay at the Empress until Wed. morning and then go to Vancouver for a day or so. I must write to Ailsa Lodge for Sat. night so I do hope to see you. Dad was at Bert's most of the time he did not get your letter very soon as it was at Jim's for a day. They forgot to take it. Did I tell you Frances has passed for a Commission and will go into the training class soon. They could not spare her for this class, had nobody to take her place, she is getting her uniform I believe and she is training a girl now, so good for Frances. Dad has gone to bed and I am tired too but thought I must get a line off to you. I will send the cookies tomorrow or Monday so excuse the delay as I can't help it. I will be able to give you fruit when you get home. How is the cash? I guess you can hang out until I get there if not let me know if you are hard up. I have not written Frances this week. I had to go to the shop one afternoon to help Jack as he was on a court case being chosen for a Coroner's Inquest so I have been busy but I have not killed myself -just kept out of mischief.

I made Miles and Barry each a nice blazer, quite smart, a stripe flannel for school, so they go off looking very nice. I will still have to keep sewing some to have them smart as nobody else seems to do anything. They knit thank goodness as I can't do that. Well Bill I will give you the news when you come or I go. As I can't think of anymore just now so will say good night.

I will write again soon

I have just got the eats ready so will have to-day Saturday

With heaps of love

From us all

Mother

S.D. Treadgold
Kelowna, B.C.

Sept 12th / 43

Dear Bill –

Well, I got your box off yesterday so hope you have received it and that the same will be edible.

Did I tell you Frances is getting her commission and will be going to officer training class before long, she has passed the test and going before the board of officers. Bill I said in my last letter to you Wilma could go to the Ludlows, well Dad said she could but he never asked them so don't say anything as he will have to make that arrangement when the time comes.

This has been a grand day and we were working around the back yard getting ready for a load of shale tomorrow. I have not sent the paper yet as I kept it for Dad to see. The kids love the pup Dad brought back with him, it is a nice little thing and so quiet. It surely is cute. They are going to call it "Kerry" or "Kerry Blue".

Both the kids are off to school now so the days will seem longer. Mr. Parker at Westbank died yesterday in Vancouver after an operation. Mrs. Ryan phoned me.

Miles was over for breakfast and wanted to come for dinner but Jack wouldn't let him however I put his dinner in the oven and he had it anyway but he didn't come for supper. He is still as hard as nails. I took the three of them to Sunday School this morning.

I have very little news Bill but hope to see you before too long. I have put your cheques in the Bank, Bill and have kept everything up to date.

Harold was here with the kids most of the day and is as ever. I think Dad is going to have a talk with him before too long.

The nights are quite cold and it is quite warm in the day.

Mr. Pettigrew is still quite sick with specials in hospital. He got out once and went in swimming which was a foolish thing to do. Mrs. Pettigrew has been discharged; she could not carry on with his illness.

I have just written Frances; she will be looking for it.

The kids went in for a swim to-day. I expect it will be the last this year. They did not dip but once.

Well Bill this is all for now very little news but you will see we are fine and Dad says he was disappointed he did not see you, better luck next time.

So with love

      Mother

Monday morn.

Just had a letter from Wilma quite a nice one, so that sounds better. She hopes to be home soon and wants me to see her next week.

                          J.H. Bowes
                      CHILLIWACK, B.C.

               September 16, 1943
R143019 - Cpl. Treadgold, W.O.
R.C.A.F. Station,
Patricia Bay, B.C.

Dear Cpl. Bill:

I was very much pleased to get your letter and find that you are well and hope to see you soon. Mrs. Ford has had two letters from Earl Brown lately. He is in Africa as you probably know, also you likely saw the distinction which Arthur Mellen has won. He is in Vancouver at present but has to go about on crutches. He is now D.F.C. and Flying Officer.

If you get into Victoria you might call on Colonel Goodland who is an intimate friend of mine. I think he is head of a Clothes Pressing Establishment, so he will welcome you for my sake.

Good news and very best wishes.

    Yours very truly,

        J.H. BOWES

Per JHB / ef

S.D. Treadgold
Kelowna, B.C.

Sept 25th / 43

Dear Bill –

Just a line to let you know I hope to be in Victoria Sunday leaving Vancouver on the Sunday morning boat, so if you could meet me, it would be nice and as I intended to go over on the night boat I did not reserve a room for Sunday night. I am booked at The Empress for Monday and Tuesday so if you will reserve a room for Sunday either The Empress or some place else, I don't mind it will be better than taking a chance.

Mr. Barton wrote and reserved a room with a bath for his two days, but as I leave earlier that will not be enough and then you can stay with me any-where you like.

I leave here on the 24th taking a sleeper from Penticton and will see Wilma on the Saturday.

We are all fine. The weather is very nice but cold at night. I may bring the papers with me. I want to leave things as good as I can for Dad and the kids. I want to get this off in the mail now. Thanks for the letter. So this is short, will give you the news when I come but I expect to write again.

With my love

Mother

S.D. Treadgold
Kelowna, B.C.
Oct 6th / 43

Dear Bill —

Well how are you tonight. We are fine and all in bed but Dad and I. Grandpa's here and Barry was sick last night and to-day but is much improved tonight, so I suppose we will get some sleep tonight.

Wilma seems better here not so restless as on Sunday and she is sleeping well so perhaps she will keep on improving. Dad seems to think her better for the time anyway. One is afraid to say much.

The weather is fine in fact grand. I have just written Frances; she will be wondering what has happened to me.

I got a grand picture of Frances in the parade in Ottawa. She looks nice walking second, looks like her.

Frances Treadgold – 2nd in line

Elmer Gutpell is in Regina now for a course and then he may go to the Coast. I had a letter from him, I have his address. He seems to like the Navy.

I have been busy since returning but feel better after the change. It was too bad Barry had to be sick last night and to-day, we had little sleep last night so I am just a little tired. Wilma slept so well on the train and she was very good indeed.

Mrs. Ryle (Apartments) died to-day I think. I have not been out so have not much news for you at this time, but I hope you got back fine and will write more when my brain is not tired although I feel fine – perhaps drop a line to-morrow

So with love

Mother

Thurs. noon...

Lovely day and you will be sorry to hear Garnet Herbert is missing and Page Robinson killed - has just been made known. Well, I will get this in the mail. Hope you are fine and write soon.

With love

Mother

S.D. Treadgold

Kelowna, B.C.

Oct 11th / 43

Dear Bill-

Your most welcome letter received to-night and how nice too, congratulations – whether it becomes final or not mum is the word. All have gone to bed so thought I would drop a line and finish tomorrow. The weather is nice sort of raining to-day and cooler tonight but we have not had a bad frost yet.

Jack got a deer or rather Roy Pollard shot it. They have it in cold storage for a week, quite a nice one I believe.

Last night Bob and Hughie were up, so we had company. Alison and Jack came in too. Wilma is not too bad. It is hard to say just how she is. I don't think those treatments seem to be just what she needs. I guess nobody knows. We all got colds and of course she had to get one too. I am getting her clothes in shape and she is to have a perm on Thursday.

Grandpa leaves on Thursday eve. I must send the paper on at once.

We have the fireplace on in the day and it seems to heat the house quite nicely so far.

Frances' birthday next Sunday. I will add more tomorrow

So with lots of love,

Mother.

Wed.

Well I did not get this off. How the time does go. This is another nice day and we are all fine. I have so little news or at least can't think of much. Grandpa is all set to leave tomorrow. After getting new shoes, sweater, pants etc. he has to come to Kelowna to get his shopping done. He seems fine though. I will be looking forward to getting your letters.

To-night I have a board meeting, so must have an early supper.

Well cheer up and be good and write soon

      With much love

         Mother

                    S.D. Treadgold
                    Kelowna, B.C.

                    Oct 17th / 43

Dear Bill –

Well how are you to-night, well I hope, and possibly in Vancouver. We have had a dull wet day so we have been in the house with the fireplace. Dad was cleaning the furnace. We have kept the fire going quite a lot lately and the kids like it. They are both asleep. The three of them went to Sunday School alone on their bicycles to-day so I have them really started. They go quite regularly.

Well I am saying very little of Wilma as I have said so much before but we think her some better. She met the children at school this last week and I am going to do my best.

I mailed you the last paper yesterday. I saw Eldith Chapman one day this week. The baby looked fine but I thought her thin (Eldith).

Grandpa left for home on Thursday so I feel sort of free again, too much for me with them all. We seem to be back more normal. The weather has been very good for so late.

This is Frances' birthday. I hope she had a happy day.

I hear Alison's father is Major now. Jack was on the sick list yesterday but is some better to-day. We had a pheasant to-day, Jack got it on Friday. Jack is pretty good he keeps giving us something which is much appreciated.

I must get busy this week and do cookies as yet I have not had a minute.

It's just 9 o'clock. We had an early supper and as nobody was in - the night seems longer.

I have so little news. Grandpa bought himself a new sweater and pants, shoes before he left. We told him to come to Kelowna to do his shopping. He has not changed any. I think he enjoyed the change but was glad to be going again.

Miles built a boat of some kind took it to the lake yesterday but of course it leaked. He is a corker but he surely is a worker, he should have a work-shop. He is always making something. His teacher likes him. Really he is an absolute scream.

Monday noon -

Well I have just received a sweater for Donna from Frances. She seems to find time for a little knit-ting. It is very nicely done.

The weather is fine and trying to dry up some. I am going to mail this now. It is just one o'clock.

Well write soon and hope you are well.

    With lots of love

       Mother

                  S.D. Treadgold
                  Kelowna, B.C.

                  Oct 26th 1943

Dear Bill −

Well Bill I have just come in from the Air Force party concert held in the school. Hundreds were turned away and it was so good. Really grand for a change. I met your friend Dug Prior and he played so well. The whole concert was quite worth while. Dug asked for you and said he had not seen you for months. I happened to be at the school for the first time for months and who should be there but the boys getting ready and I looked around and saw Dug. He was so surprised to see me. He said he saw the store and felt like going in so I told him to go in and see Jack. I hope he does but his time is short as they leave to-morrow at 9 A.M. I asked him to the house but that is out of the question as his time is all taken up with supper, dance, concert etc. However I surely enjoyed it and I would not have been there had it not been for Dug as he asked me if I was not going so I decided to go.

The weather is quite mild. You will be looking for a letter but of course I have been busy and read for a while on Sunday when I should have written and Frances too, she will wonder.

I have not sent the suit yet. It is all ready and the shirt too but the skates Dad will have to see which pair. I was saying today I will have to get at cookies as I said before. I hope to have more time as Wilma is helping more now. I think Wilma better and will tell you the whole story some day when she recovers, which I say she will do so for the present I say very little. Just keep on. You will be glad you have no trips to make, as it surely was a chore. I am going to write Frances a line. She goes into the training class for 3 weeks on the 14th however and after that it will be the West or the East, probably the East she said. She spent Saturday in Montreal so that would be a change. Colie Campbell has been transferred to Vancouver but is here now. A young airman I forgot his name, nice looking, was over Germany and Africa etc. gave quite a talk to-night, telling all about the dangers etc. If you get through, he says you are lucky. The worst is to see all your pals killed. Very few get through 60 raids. They do 30 raids and then rest for a time 6 months no more and no more than 60. Mrs. Lingly sat beside me. I felt very sorry for her. She is a brick through.

Well Bill I hope you are not put out waiting a few days for the suit. I will send it right away. Dad is very busy and is trying to get a man or so if possible. We had a couple of days rain and what a mess. It is after ten so by the time I write Frances I will want to go to bed.

Dug was telling me they were going to take all the W.D.s [Women Division] out of Pat Bay (so he heard). I hope you are getting on fine and I am sure you are. Write soon and give me all the news. So Bye Bye for now.

     With my love

          Mother

                         S.D. Treadgold
                         Kelowna, B.C.

                         Nov 3rd 1943

Dear Bill —

Well Bill it is time I was writing you again and also to get the paper off.

I sent the suit, shirt, skates so hope you received them. The weather is fine and dried up some and all the leaves are nearly down so it is more like winter but it is not cold.

I received the letter telling of Talking to The Wrens. I have not heard from Frances for awhile but I expect she is fine, also Jim.

The kiddies are fine and Donna seems to be growing up. I think she has a long way to walk at noon for the little bit she eats. Dad usually takes her back but it is a long walk. To-day a boy gave her a nasty crack with a shiv on the forehead, quite a nasty one; what these kids don't do.

We will soon be having snow by the look of the weather but I hope it does not get too cold. Dad is quite busy and has a new man on.

So, you met the Board: well, I expect it was quite an experience anyway. I wish this old war would finish up and let people live again. I was raking up a few leaves to-day but there are still quite a few left.

I started to make cookies to-day but did not seem to make a lot of headway, so perhaps to-morrow I will do better. I will try and send you some very soon. The days seem to go so quickly. The house is nice and warm, almost too much but we let the furnace out at night.

I have very little news but we are all fine and I hope you are too and I am always so glad to get you letters. I am always looking forward to mail and I expect you are too. I hope I sent the right skates. Jack has been playing at the odd dance lately.

Miles goes to school on his bike so I don't see quite so much of him but I still do see him and he is quite a boy. Dad says it is raining now. It seems to rain at night.

Well Bill I may add some more to-morrow and I will get you some cookies off I am sorry to be so slow but write soon.

So will say Goodnight

      With lots of love

          Mother

Thursday noon

Dear Bill

Well I don't seem to have anymore news Bill but this is a nice day and drying up. It is really nice - I was uptown for a few moments. I am sending in

last weeks paper and will send this week's tomorrow if all see it by then.

Hope you are fine, so bye bye for now

Mother

S.D. Treadgold
Kelowna, B.C.

Nov 9th 1943

Dear Bill -

Your letter received today and glad you are feeling
better again. We are all as usual and the weather
is nice and everyone seems busy.

When I got home from town at five Donna had started
to set the table, she is quite a girl, the life of
the party. She is growing up fast, she can read and
is very proud of it, she is not helpless.

Joyce Cattee - did she give the family a surprise. I
hope he is nice. Mr. Chamberlain died from a stroke
and was buried on Sunday. Jack has been playing at
dances lately, I expect that drummers are scarce.

I sent you a box of eats on Saturday - hope you
received them.

To-morrow I have a board meeting. I had a letter
from Frances and she wasn't very well for a few
days but is fine again. She has her Xmas shopping
done and expects to be busy when she goes in the
O.T.C. [Officers Training Corps] which lasts 3
weeks. I have not written Jim nor have I heard from
them. I must write them perhaps they will answer.
I go up town so little that really I don't seem to

gather much news. Dad has been up at the shop a few nights getting some pictures done. I expect he too is thinking of Xmas. Did you hear a rebroadcast of Churchill's speech today? He thinks the war will finish next year with the worst to come.

I think the weather this fall is better than last. The leaves are still coming down and it has dried up quite well.

The pup is growing up too and what a dog to eat. He keeps Dad busy 3 times a day looking for food. Well Bill this is all for to-night. Write soon, so hope you are fine and that all is well

With lots of love

    As ever

       Mother

               S.D. Treadgold
               Kelowna, B.C.

               Nov 17th 1943

Dear Bill –

Well here it is Wed. afternoon and a very nice day. Yesterday it seemed cold but to-day it looks nice. Wilma has gone to meet the children and I may go up town after I write you.

I received your letter written from Vancouver where the welcome in the mat is not so prominent some times at least for me, but you – that is different. You want to take no notice or they would forget what I look like so put your feelings in your pocket sometimes, however I hope they are both well. I have been wondering why Jim is not medically fit. It may be his arm or eyes. Vie is surely furry at times and nice at times too; just now I expect she is not quite herself. We are all fine and busy as usual. It seems hard to get all in at times but we manage fine.

I had a letter from Frances and she is not going in the training class until the end of January as they have a new unit of officers and it would be too much to let her go now. She said she did not know she was so important but she did not care at all and perhaps it would be best after Xmas and I expect she will know where she will be for Xmas. She was asking for 10 days next month and was going to visit Millie, Willo also Annie in Kitchener and get her Officer's uniform from the Tip Top in Toronto as Ottawa is not so good she said and I have to send her a dress and shoes so she can change, officers can change some times.

So you saw Dug Prior. He said he liked Kelowna, most people seem to and they seem to be coming in still.

Barry has just come in. He has new shoes and is taking them off although he likes them. This is the first day so I expect his feet to change. Donna got some too but did not wear hers to-day.

I have done up the paper, forgot I had not sent it.

I suppose Joyce is staying with Vie. I surely don't get much news, only what you send, so many thanks. Well Bill I think I will try and get this in the mail. I hope you are fine and don't worry, things won't last for ever. That's what I always say so cheer up and write soon.

With heaps of love

    As ever

        Mother

                        Mr. J.H. Bowes
                        Chilliwack, B.C.

                        November 18, 1943

R143019 Cpl. Treadgold, W.O
R.C.A.F. Station,
Patricia Bay, B.C.

Dear Bill:

I was more than pleased to get your letter which quite cheered me up. I hope that Commission will come along soon and by all means take it if you get the chance.

The Ford house is full of young soldiers who are at work on army vehicles and cars. They are all quiet and have very little to say. I miss the old gang of bank clerks.

There is no news here. I might state that I am still wearing the tie you gave me some four years ago. It must have been of the very best material.

I am looking forward to seeing you and we will have a dinner at the Peak's where I suppose you still know all of the pretty waitresses.

Best wishes, I remain,

    Yours very sincerely,

        JHB/ef   J.H. Bowes

L.E. Gutpell.
H.M.C.S. Queen
Regina, Sask.,

Nov. 23, 1943.

Dear Bill:

Not having heard from you I had imagined you were posted elsewhere. However, I'm glad you are still at Pat Bay because I'm looking forward to seeing you soon.

For a long while we expected to be posted to Halifax but it now seems we are coming to Esquimalt and unless there are any sudden changes, we will leave here on the 28th.

Have been hoping to visit Vancouver, etc. for a long, long time, dating back to civilian days. Finally, I'm within striking distance. Come to think of it I've been in over 5 months now - seems a long time.

The last three weeks my social life has been nil here. There are some fine young ladies here but on an average and taking a standard, I think London, Ontario has 'em beat. I understand Vancouver is in a class by itself and I'm counting on doing the bright spots with you.

Had a note from Lt. Jack Palframan at Givenchy [HMCS Givenchy was a naval class trawler constructed for the Royal Canadian Navy as an accommodation ship during WW2 - Wikipedia]. Have you seen him at all?

Things are about the same back home. Dad is busy and Mother worries as much as ever. Young John is talking about buying diamond rings and I'm still absolutely neutral about that phase of life. Maybe I'm not the type! I like a good time, luxuries, and lots of $$$$. Maybe I'll change though, as all my friends have been working on me.

Have been hearing regularly from my top three bosses back at Forsyth's and often wish I was there again, even though I like the Navy. They are a grand firm to work for.

Have a good cold in my system and ache a bit here and there. We should go on draft leave tomorrow night and I'll get it cleared up then for sure and quickly. The Forsyth trav. here and myself are going to Moose Jaw and while I'm not a drinking man I'm willing to make exceptions for medicinal reasons!!!!

Will write you when I hit next ship,

  Best regards,

   Elmer

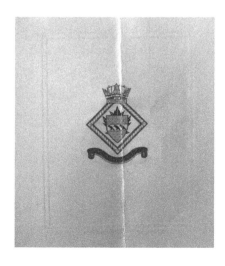

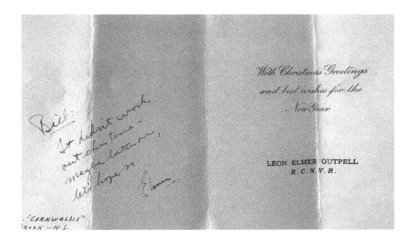

With Christmas Greetings
and best wishes for the
New Year

LEON ELMER GUTPELL
R.C.N.V.R.

Bill:
It didn't work
out this time -
maybe later on,
let's hope so.
Elmer.

"CORNWALLIS"
ROOK - N.S.

S.D. Treadgold
Kelowna, B.C.

Nov 25th 1943

Dear Bill –

Well Bill I must get a note off to you to-day to wish you Many Happy Returns of your birthday. We are all fine except Barry and he was on the sick list yesterday and today but not too bad. I had to change my program today, as Miss Tilling phoned to say I could have a perm today so it makes me rush as I had not expected until next week. However I will be glad to get it over. I have been cooking and it is near lunch time. I am wondering when you may be home or will it be Xmas. The weather has been grand, more like spring. Jim phoned last Wed night a week ago to say they have a daughter, but that's all we heard so I expect they are fine.

Dad was able to get a bicycle for Barry. It has just been made up of parts but fine indeed. He has not been on it yet. Donna goes to school on hers now, she looks so cute and so tiny on it but it is quite a help in getting her there.

Barry, Donna and Miles on their bikes

Miles wants a big one now, he is getting larger every day. I will have to rush as I have to be up town at one o'clock. I am not sending you much for your birthday but will enclose $1 just to let you know I have not forgotten.

I received your letter a day or so ago where you might be home and I sent two papers, I believe I sent a paper just before that, I had sent one like it as I so seldom have an extra paper, I never looked at the date so I hope you can make out what I am talking about.

    With heaps of love and best wishes

    Mother

Just received a letter from Jim, all is well

S.D. Treadgold
Kelowna, B.C.

Dec 2nd 1943

Dear Bill –

Your most welcome letter received to-night written after being in Vancouver. Well, you seem to stick to Pat Bay fairly well and I expect one could do much worse.

I had a letter from Frances too and she said she forgot your birthday until she wrote the date that day. She seems fine and always so busy. She says the only way to get a rest is to clear out but she seems quite happy.

Well Barry has a fair size bicycle now so he is happy too and they both go to school on their bicycles. It sort of gives Dad a rest. He is getting busy for Xmas. In one of your letters you said something about working for Dad. Well Dad said he could surely use you so time will tell what may turn up. Dad is up town for awhile to-night. It is just seven o'clock. We have supper after five so it makes the evening long.

You will be surprised to hear that Mr. Arbuckle died at the first of the week in Essendale and was buried to-day. He was to have come home I believe and then took a bad turn and died soon. I expect it is better for Mrs. Arbuckle than to have that held over her, perhaps for a long time.

The weather has been very grand. I was thinking to-day I must get you some cookies off right away. Jack got a nice 2 point deer on Sunday. He seems to like hunting. So by your letter Jim and Vie have called their baby Trudy which is very nice.

Dad is quite busy. It seems to come, now, he is doing pictures for Xmas. He seems to line up the stock and they get picked up. I think he is going to have his teeth out soon.

I have not sent you last week's paper although I have it all ready it has been on the table for a couple of days. I sent the children over the way with a paper and they came back with the paper around it in their hand so I never tried that again but will get it off tomorrow and perhaps this week's if Dad brings it home tonight.

Well you seem to get your weekends and I think you would miss them if they should end.

Bob comes to see us each week and is coming on Sunday to take some snaps of the kiddies and the wonderful dog. He is a fright to keep in – a real jumper etc. and he likes tearing up my porch Lino. The house seems quite warm to-night. I was up at the school to visit. Barry's home today for a few minutes. It was Open Day for him so I could not disappoint him and I went to see Donna too. She can read now and is doing quite well. She is going to be a great girl. I would have liked to have seen Miles too but I did not have time today, will again.

I must drop Frances a line she will be on leave soon I think she said she would let me know when.

Why did Joan come back to Vancouver? Has her husband been moved? Mr. Little told dad he flew to Vancouver with you, I saw him yesterday. I think the Anglican Bazaar is open tomorrow so I may go there for awhile. They still have them. It will be very nice if you can get home for Xmas but we are glad to have you any time. I will drop Frances a line now and then add to this if I have any more later

So Bye Bye for now

    Mother

Bill - you will be sorry to hear Colin Byer is missing over Germany Nov 23rd

Friday- Have just got the cookies packed and ready for mail, so here's hoping they are fine.

Love - Mother

                          S.D. Treadgold
                          Kelowna, B.C.

                          Dec 10th 1943

Dear Bill -

Your most welcome letter received today, short but welcome indeed. I intended writing the last few nights but between one thing or another. The children both have had the flu I think as they got better and then went down again in a few days however. I think it is over again as Donna is much better to-day. It is quite a lot of work looking after them when sick and sort of makes one tired. Miles is off colour to-day so I expect he is the same. Donna had a high temperature yesterday.

The weather is very nice and I am ready for you if you come. Dad is going into hospital on Monday to have his teeth out. He is feeling quite good but his teeth worry him and his nose has not been too good so I will be glad when that clears up.

Different ones have been asking if you are coming home. You will see lots of changes as that seems to be the majority when I go uptown.

Donna is going to the dentist at nine in the morning she had a little toothache from one that was filled awhile ago. Barry has lost most of his front teeth, has one lone one by itself and it looks funny.

We will be glad to have you home again.

Sat. morning

I have just been uptown for a few minutes. Dad says when he is home next week he may be lying around for a few days. Then I will get all my shopping finished. These days it takes so long to get what you want. The weather is frosty at night but quite nice in fact we have had the best fall yet. I have very little news but will do the paper up and get it off with this letter so hoping to see you before long and we will try and have a nice Xmas.

So bye bye with love

    As ever

        Mother

CHAPTER SIX
1944

Pat Bay - Things were going badly with the War. Troops from everywhere were being shipped regularly to England depleting the bases of man power. The RCAF sent in "gals" - the gals came in to replace many of the men going overseas. "We felt threatened by the women – but by God I took to this one beautiful girl and I said this is the girl I want to marry."

December 31 - Dad proposes to Irene Bell. "The greatest day of my life was in 1944 New Year's Eve in Victoria. They had just turned the lights on at the Parliament Buildings (four years without light due to war). There wasn't a soul there except for Irene and me. I went into OB

Allan on Granville in Vancouver and spent $75 for the ring" (notes from interview of Bill by Cathie Pavlik, 2008).

Doris Irene Bell

GLOBAL EVENTS TIMELINE - 1944

27 January - Russians broke the siege of Leningrad

12 March - German troops invaded Hungary

23 May - Successful Canadian assault on the Hitler Line

4 June - Americans liberate Rome, 15 000 Canadians land at Normandy

13 June - First V-1 falls on London, US wins Battle of Philippine Seas

4 September - British capture Antwerp

9 September - Bulgaria declares war on Germany

12 September – Canadians were to clear the Scheldt

23-26 October – The U.S. Pacific Fleet Japanese crushed at Leyte Gulf

28 November - Canadians successful at Scheldt

16 December - Germans launch Battle of the Bulge

https://www.mta.ca/library/courage/worldwariichronology.html cited May 29, 2021

OUR FILE......................................

REF. YOUR.....................................

DATED...

ROYAL CANADIAN AIR FORCE

Patricia Bay, B.C.,
February 1,1944.

Dear Barry:-

I was very very glad to get your letter and also Donnas'. Thankyou very much kids.

I'm a very poor typist but will endeavour to pound out a few words to you while I am at the office. I had to come back and work for awhile.

How is everything there with you both....... and please say "Hello" to Miles for me. I think about you young rascals a lot and I wish I could be there in your fun. How is school?????? I learn Donna that you are starting to dance -- that's pretty swell I think. I'll take you to the first dance next time I'm home. Is this a date?

How is your bike Barry and are you keeping it in good running order? How is the tool - box progressing too? I am sending you a couple of things here for your collection. This is for your birthday by the way. I know you have one this month - but I'm just not sure of the date. Anyhow Many Happy Returns for the BIG day to come.

I've been working pretty hard this week and it appears that I'll be this way for awhile too. Though I expect to leave here soon for somewhere I don't know.

SAY -------------------- ARE YOU BRUSHING YOUR TEETH EVERY DAY ????????? You promised me you would twice every day, so please don't forget.I suppose you are getting your new teeth in about now Barry. Look after them.

Well, it is time I left here for barracks. I'ts 8:30 and I have some washing to do and must iron my uniform. You should be tucked in bed by now. So until I write again - be good kids please. When you can write me again for I'll be ever so pleased to hear from you. Don't forget to say "Hello" to Miles and tell him to write me too.

Cheerio Barry and Donna ....

Love,

Uncle Bill

R.C.A.F. G. 32
9500M—8-42 (2401)
H.Q. 885-G-92

Letter from Bill to Barry and Donna

"Keep in touch with the folks at home"

ON ACTIVE SERVICE
WITH THE
CANADIAN FORCES

K-20 Krasselt A.W.
H.Q.Sqn. 9th Arm'd Regt. (B.C.D.)
Cdn. Army (C.M.F.)

25 Feb, 1944

Dear Oscar:

Many thanks for your swell letter of Dec 22 received some time ago. Should have and would have answered sooner but time does not give us much chance to do much writing now that we are over here.

Your stay in Kelowna sounds terrific. Could really go for a leave there myself — that will be the day. Oh for a dance in the IOOF Hall or Aquatic Club.

Re Edith Bill the name is not yet Krasselt, but if I am fortunate enough to get back to Blighty it certainly will be. Thanks for all your good wishes Bill.

Had a letter from Joyce C the other day and she seems to be very well and quite busy. She did have a rather close shave and as you say — Thank God she was saved.

Glad to hear you had an enjoyable evening at home Bill. Guess Mom and Dad did miss us all this year. Guess will have to make it a family reunion next Xmas. What a hope!!

The weather over here is far from Sunny these days. Instead, it's rain, snow and hail making mud knee deep. Am away from the Unit at the moment, but hope to be back with the gang very soon.

Not much else to say Bill, so will sign off.

Hoping that this finds you as well as it leaves me, and that you'll drop me a line again soon.

Until then, this is all best wishes and good luck Bill.

Sincerely

    your chum

        Krass

                J.H. BOWES
              CHILLIWACK, B.C.

               March 9, 1944

R143019 - Cpl.
Treadgold, W.O.,
R.C.A.F. Station,
Patricia Bay, B.C.

Dear Bill:

I was very pleased to hear from you and indeed was wondering why I had not heard from you before this.

I was hoping that you would be able to get to Chilliwack also to find that you were now a Sgt. or still better an officer, but perhaps this will come later.

WENDY HAMILTON & CATHERINE PAVLIK

Yes, I will be in Victoria quite soon and shall make it a point to let you know where to find me when I get there.

I met Douglas Monteith some weeks ago and he was very helpful in getting me to a place when I had lost my way. He is a fine chap.

I hope your mother and all the family are in the best of health, you might remember me to her when you next write.

Now I am looking forward to seeing you either here in Chilliwack or in Victoria quite soon.

   Yours very truly,

    JHB/ef   J.H.Bowes

        S.D. Treadgold
        Kelowna, B.C.

        April 16th 44

Dear Bill -

Well Bill Donna received her dolls. They are indeed very nice. Donna likes them. Thank Pat for me and Donna will write her a line. They are beautifully made. This is a nice day but it has been quite frosty at nights. We have part of our garden planted; Frances was going to Kitchener for her 48hrs this weekend. She seems fine. They had quite a blizzard there on Good Friday but it was nice before that. I forgot to say Bob is coming up tonight. Dad and I are going to the Maxims for awhile. I must send you the paper with this letter and I guess I had better get a box of cookies off. We will all be glad when

202

it gets a little warmer. I have not had the furnace on so the house is none too warm. The children are out playing. Barry surely plays better than he did. He is still without Insulin but we are not quite sure yet, he may have to have a little but I hope not.[xxiii] School to-morrow again. There is a new house going up opposite Jack's on the corner. I don't know who owns it yet. Miles was here for breakfast came about 7:15 and stayed for lunch but he is off this afternoon. He comes almost every Sunday morning.

The guests are buying Mrs. Maxim a silver tea service, very nice. I see by the Province one of the Pearson's boys from Glenmore is missing. I believe his brother was either missing or killed before. I will finish this later —

Monday morn. Another nice day. The party is over and it was quite nice. They gave them a large silver tray. I thought it was to be a tea service but it is very nice. Bill don't say too much to Isobel as Wilma would have to be a little better than she is at times before she could go anywhere but under somebody's care. I will write you again soon. I washed this morning so have kept busy today. I will put this and the paper in the mail. Hope you are fine. So with heaps of love

As ever

    Mother

       Write soon

S.D. Treadgold
Kelowna, B.C
April 27th 44

Dear Bill –

Well here it is Thursday again and another nice day. I was uptown this morning and mailed a box of eats to you, so you may get them before this letter. I wrote Jim had a nice letter from him. Vie, Joyce, Lonnie and Trudy were here on Sunday for the day. Trudy is a dear. She is so tiny and so good. I fell in love with her. I am sorry to hear of Bert. Wilma was terrible on Sunday when Vie was here. She seems worse, if that can be, when anyone is around.

The kids are fine and full of beans. They will be writing you soon. I got a new bottle of ink so this will be a little better, I hope.

I hear that the other Herbert boy, I expect is Ralph, is missing. Garnet was killed some time ago.

Dad keeps very busy and is still turning down work. Vie seems to want to come back to Kelowna too so I would not be surprised if they do in time. I must do a little gardening to-day. Some of the seeds are coming up and such a lot of flowers mean I could be getting an armful or more.

I have not a lot of news. I keep too busy to gather news. Everybody seems to be in the gardens. Although I don't seem to do much, my spring garden is the best I have seen.

Sylvia Maud Roxby fell off her horse on Tues. night and received bad head injuries.

Barry has joined the Cubs and seems to be quite
happy over it and is looking forward to getting
a uniform. He has made up at school so the report
says. It is easy for him to learn and he remembers
so well. He was telling about the bombs he saw on
the army train and we had forgotten it. Miles is
still going strong. Violet thought they had grown
so, she had not seen them for quite a time.

There seem to be quite a lot of people coming to
town from the prairies, such a lot of strangers
to us.

I think I will go in the sunshine for awhile and if
I don't get this mailed to-day may add some more.
Glad you are fine in the office.

Friday noon.

Dear Bill - another nice day, am going up town to
do shopping but I have no more news. Will write
soon. Hope you are well. I will send the paper
on soon.

So bye bye

        With love

            Mother

                        S.D. Treadgold
                        Kelowna, B.C.

                        May 3rd / 44

Dear Bill,

Well Bill just a line to thank you for the nice
box of candy. I have not had much candy of late

so it is appreciated all the more. We are all fine and the weather is very nice, getting warmer and bright sunshine.

Dad has the boat painted and I suppose it is all ready for the lake as he put the name on it last night. He still keeps busy. We all keep busy thank goodness.

I had a letter from Frances and she is fine. She has not asked off yet but by her letter I would not be surprised if she gets home a little later. It will soon be a year since she was here.

I met Mr. DeLong also Mr. Ford yesterday and Mr. Lord's daughter Eleanor was asking about you. I think she was on the train at Xmas time when you were. Ray Herbert is alright I think there was a mistake. It was a Herbert from Kamloops missing so I expect the Herberts here were relieved.

I will have to get busy and get something done around here before Frances arrives, although things are not bad.

Dad is sleeping on the porch but it is cool at night. Mrs. Billy Pettigrew is building on the corner lot opposite Jack so Abbott St. is building up. Houses are very few here now. Dad will tell you - the Maxims are going to live in Jones' boat house for the summer.

I will soon have to get busy with lunch, the time seems to fly. I sent you the paper so most of the news will be there. Well Bill, write soon. I hope you are well and getting on fine. Will add more later if it comes to my mind.

So with my love

Mother

Dear Bill -

I received your letter today noon. It is now nearly one o'clock. I sent you a box of cookies which I thought you would get by Saturday hope you get them and that the pies aren't mouldy. I will get this in the mail box. I got some purple dye to dye some wool to mend your sweaters, the one you left seems to have some holes, however I will fix them. I tried every store in town for wool and not any at all, so will make some. It is hot now and I must hurry again. I did pretty good this A.M. went to town etc.

Well, write soon.

With heaps of love and again thanks for the chocolates

Mother

J. H. Bowes,

Chilliwack, B.C.

June 2, 1944

R143019 Cpl.
Treadgold, W.D.,
R.C.A.F. Station,
Patricia Bay, B.C.

Dear Bill:

It was very pleasant to get a letter from you and I am sorry indeed that we will not be able to meet in Vancouver or anywhere else unless you take a flying trip to Toronto where I expect to go in a few days. I do not know how long I will be there and if I don't like it I will come back to the West but whether to Chilliwack or not is another question. Of course, if Mrs. Ford had not quit, I don't think I would have gone but after all it is only about 2400 miles so the journey won't matter very much.

I certainly hope to see you some time either in Toronto or after I return to the West. You can always get me by writing to 310 Bloor St. West, Toronto, Can.

Kind regards to your Mother. As to the Bible I hope you read it.

Yours very truly,

J.H. Bowes.
Per EF

KJB/ef

K-20 Krasselt A.W.
HQ Sqn. 9th A.R. (B.C.D.)
Cdn Army (C.M.F.)

26 June 44

Hello Oscar:

Many thanks for your two swell letters of June 12 — one air— received together this evening. Yes, Bill it is quite a while since I last wrote to you, but I hope you will understand when I say that I've been too busy to do much writing. The SSM has been away and I got saddled with his duties as well as my own so time has been very scarce.

Expect to be going on a 72 hr leave to a rest camp situated on a nice sandy beach of the blue Med sometime this week. Also expect an 8 day soon. This also will be spent at a similar camp. Sure hope the weather stays fine so that I'll be able to get in some swimming and take in a load of sunshine.

Guess maybe you will be interested to know what I think of the Capital City. Well Bill it is really something for Italy and far different from any other town or city I've seen over here. It's a very clean city with wide streets—very nice buildings and for a change the people are well dressed and look half way intelligent. Course time was short so I didn't see as much of it as I would have liked to. However maybe I'll get a chance again sometime.

There you go again Bill losing the big ones. Bet you were mad when you lost 14 lbs of delicious fish.

So you haven't got a gal down that way any more eh Bill — you must be slipping. I'm in the same fix cause now I'm over here — but just wait 'till I set down in "Blighty" again.

The weather was quite fine here again today after a terrific storm over the weekend. The rain came down in sheets and the wind drove it in both ends of our open tent and also through the roof. We were literally swimming inside as we stood holding the tent and poles so it wouldn't blow away — some fun. We're all dried out again now and anyway we're getting quite used to these sorts of things.

Must close now Bill. Thanks again for your swell letters and — don't go doing anything that I wouldn't.

Au revoir with all best wishes and good luck.

    Your Pal

       Krass & Alban

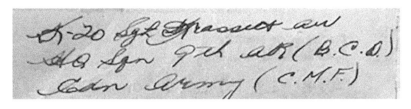

K-20 Krasselt A.W.
HQ Sqn. 9th A.R. (B.C.D.)
Cdn Army (C.M.F.)

24 Aug 1944

Dear Bill:

Many thanks "Reed" for your two welcome letters of July 16 and Aug 6 which arrived recently. Sorry to be so late in answering but I just couldn't settle down to it, especially when there is so little news. You seem to be doing O.K. in the Hostess Club in Victoria — ever meet a gal by the name of Joan Glendenning — or Rose Leuschen? 'Cause it's over 3 years since I had a go in the club, but they used to be there quite often. Very nice too.

Sure sorry to hear about Norah Perry. She was a swell kid too.

It's still very hot over here and close too. Gosh we just drip all day and half the night. However, we'll get used to it.

Hope to visit Eldith's native land soon and maybe even see her home town. So hold everything 'cause here we come!!

Wonder where we'll spend Xmas this year. Some say at home, but I have my doubts. Course the news is very grand - I hope it's soon better. Who knows

—maybe we'll spend the big day in Berlin or gay Paris. Wos Wos — that will be the day.

Had a letter from Eldith the other day and she seems to be quite well and the same old Eldith.

Expect to see a show in camp tonight so will have to rush and get all my letters answered before dark — hence this terrible scribble.

Well Oscar old dear this seems to be all for Now. Will see you up at Beaver Lake next summer — O.K.

Until next time Bill — be good or if you can't do that be careful. Hoping that this finds you as well as it leaves me.

Au revoir

    Your chump

        Krass

190 Lowther Ave.,
Toronto, Ontario.
December 15th,44.

Sgt. W. Treadgold,
R.C.A.F. Patricia Bay,
Vancouver Island, B.C.

Dear Bill:

I have not heard from you for ages nore has Mrs.
Ford, but I suppose you did not know where to address me.

I will be here at 190 Lowther Avenue, until the
end of the month and after that may return to Chilliwack but
a letter addressed to Lowther Avenue will be forwarded to me.

I am glad to know you are a full-fledged Sgt.
now. Please remember me to your mother and any friends you
may happen to see.

Yours sincerely,

J. H. Bowes.

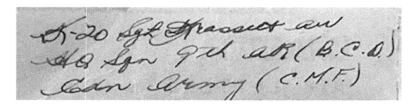

K-20 Krasselt A.W.
HQ Sqn. 9th A.R. (B.C.D.)
Cdn Army (C.M.F.)

28 Dec 44

Dear Bill:

Many thanks for your welcome letter of 11 Nov or I should say Dec which I received yesterday. Pleased to hear that you're well and still going strong.

As you will note by the date Xmas is now a thing of the past and the New Year will soon be likewise. Due to the present circumstances, we were unable to have a regimental Xmas dinner. We therefore had three of them starting on the 24th and having the third one on the 26th. I ate on the 26th and really had a very nice dinner. 'Course there was lots of Xmas cheer floating around, but as my old stomach won't take it anymore, I partook of very little of it. Everyone seemed to have quite a good time though, considering everything. Guess that everyone hoped as I did though that by next year at this time we'll at least be in a country where the people speak English. A guy does pick up a bit of "Itie", but God what a treat it would be to find yourself in a country where one could speak their own language.

At the moment 7 of us are living in one room in an old Itie house. Just out behind some big guns are doing their stuff. Every time they shoot the tiles on the roof shuffle like a deck of cards and deposit all the dirt that they have gathered for the past hundred years down on our heads. However, we're lucky to be indoors and how we realize it after spending last winter in pup tents etc.

The weather here is quite cold now, but so far we haven't had any snow in this particular section.

On reading this over it sounds like one continual beef, however it certainly wasn't meant that way, so please excuse.

Will sign off now Bill, hoping that this finds you as well as it leaves me. Also wishing you nothing but the best for 1945. This is, as ever

    Your chum,

      Alban

CHAPTER SEVEN
1945

BILL'S TIMELINE - 1945

August 18 - Bill and Irene get married in Vancouver at the Holy Trinity Anglican Church on West 12th Avenue. A reception followed at Irene's family home.

Bill remains stationed in Pat Bay, B.C. until 1946

Bill and Irene posing for a street photographer in Vancouver.

GLOBAL EVENTS TIMELINE - 1945

9 January - Allied troops invade Philippines

11 January - 5304 Canadian casualties while forcing German troops across the Rhine

22 April - Russians reach Berlin; Berlin surrendered

7 May – Germany surrendered unconditionally to the Allies

8 May - VE (Victory in Europe) Day

6 August - Americans use first atomic bomb on Hiroshima

9 August - The United States dropped a second bomb on Nagasaki

10 August - Japan opened peace negotiations

14 August - Japan to an unconditional surrender

15 August - VJ (Victory in Japan)
Day

https://www.mta.ca/library/courage/worldwariichronology.html cited May 29, 2021

1348 Yonge St. Apt 98
Toronto Ontario

F. Willo Palframan
Jan 25/45

Dear Bill,

Congratulations. Your letter was rather a surprise but we were real pleased to hear from you and wish you every happiness. By all accounts you had a swell Christmas. Too bad you cannot get home more often but here's hoping the war will soon be over and everyone might be able to settle down.

Have not seen the Gutpells lately. Annie was supposed to come down about 3 weeks ago but she fell down cellar with the garbage pail on top of her and has been a little crippled since. However I think she is pretty good now. Had a letter from Elmer. He seems to be doing fine and not disliking it too much. Jack is in Sarnia now. We haven't seen him lately either but he is fine. He and Jean have had a break-up but do not know how it is going to end. Likely with the "Wedding March".

Frances was in Toronto before Christmas. I missed her, but Millie was speaking to her and says she is looking fine and enjoying Military Life.

Wilf, Muriel and Boys are as ever and so are the Heberles and Jim.

I pulled one on them this year and spent Christmas in the Hospital. Not a bad place but I would just as soon be home where can wait on yourself. I am doing fine now and I think another 2 or 3 weeks will see me back at work. Hope so anyway.

I suppose Frances has told you about all the snow we have this winter. About all the men can do is work and shovel snow. The streets are still piled high with it.

Well Bill, as you know I am no letter writer, so will close now hoping to hear from you soon, and if you have any spare snaps of the "Girl" send them along.

Best of Luck to you both.

    Love

        Willo and Millie

                S.D. Treadgold
                Kelowna, B.C.

                January 25th 1945

Dear Bill –

Your letter received regarding questions. I was a little surprised at what was on your mind. You asked for our approval. Well Bill surely you must know you have our approval as long as you both are satisfied. We are both quiet and make little fuss and you were engaged and wanted at that time to keep it quiet. We have not criticized Irene or even thought of it. She seems like a very nice girl so congratulations. I am sure Irene's mother or anybody else will not give you better wishes than from home. Irene when she comes into the family will be received just the same as the other two girls have been. We think of them as in the family and hope and trust our boys are happy and we will always treat them well.

As for keeping quiet or asking questions I really never thought of it. These things work themselves out. I don't feel it is up to me to work out their future. As for Jim you must know Jim. Violet in her letter wrote very nicely and as for Jack you know him too.

You were here such a short time we may have had our minds centered on the children and their mother, which I am sure you, or nobody, only those who have gone through it, can in the faintest degree, realize. We have tried our best to keep up in every way and hope again to have a normal life. A mental illness is not anything more to be ashamed of than other illness.

Dad says he certainly did not want to slight anybody in the slightest. You must not worry over these things. They will work out for the best when you wish it so and try to that end. It worries me when you see things this way so for goodness' sake think of home as wishing you both well and as for congratulations, I may not have used the word but

I wrote you other words. Jack and Allison were not happy for a time and it worried Dad and I very much at the time and we feel we didn't want to interfere with anybody's plans but willing at all times to give aid or advise when called on to do so. I think I should be clear. I will write Irene as I said in my last letter. It is our wish for you to be happy so forget this other stuff.

It is more than work worrying about such things. Don't get down in the dumps no matter what happens. Keep your head. I would rather you said things while here if things were not to your liking, I told Irene I would have liked to have a party or something but at this time could not manage it.

I wanted to get this off today but am not sure now I may be able to. I have had neuralgia one side of my head this week but it's some better today. Barry has been home three days. He may be in for the measles. It looks as if Jim will be in Vancouver for a time. Frances expects to go to Ottawa next month.

I will enclose a letter for you and tell Irene I will write her not today but soon.

The weather is grand. I will send the paper tomorrow.

So Bye Bye

With our love

As ever

Mother

K-20 Krasselt A.W.

H.Q.Sqn. 9th A.R. (B.C.D)

Cdn Army (C.M.F.)

28 Jan. 1945

Dear Bill:-

Many thanks Oscar for your ever welcome letter which I received at noon yesterday. First of all Bill—please accept my hearty <u>CONGRATULATIONS</u> ON YOUR BECOMING ENGAGED AND HERE'S WISHING BOTH YOURSELF AND Irene everything of the best. She must be a swell Girl Bill and She's certainly got a great guy so — lots of luck once again to you Both.

Your trip home sounds swell, and can well imagine how you enjoyed it all. Am certainly looking forward to the day when we'll all be back to that "Home Town". Can't help but think how different it will be though with so many of the old gang missing and the rest of you guys married and settled down. What in the hell will an old bachelor do with himself?

You ask about Xmas etc. Bill. Well consider-ing everything we did very well over the holiday season. We had a very nice Xmas dinner of turkey etc. and managed to scrounge enough chicken etc. to have a feed on New Years. 'Course there was plenty of "Bingo" flowing during the season which really made things merry.

At the moment we're in a back area enjoying our otherwise life in a static camp. Have had a hectic week doing a little bit of everything. First of all, the SSM was sick so I had a few days go at that. Then it was Guard Sgt and now Orderly Joe. That's what we dislike about a camp such as this. There are far more duties etc. here than when we're up the "sharp end". However, it's all in a lifetime.

Had a very nice dinner and party in the mess last night. Strictly stag of course (won't know how to act if I ever see a white woman again) but all very much enjoyed.

The weather has been quite cold with the odd flake of snow, but still much better than we had last winter.

Well Bill it looks like signing off time again so once again wishing you all the best, this is, as ever

       Your chum

         Krassy

                   F.M. Treadgold
            H.M.C.S. "Cornwallis"
              Cornwallis, N.S.

                    6th Feb. 1945.

Dear Bill

I hope the shock of receiving a letter from me will not be too much for you! 'Tis a long road that hasn't any turning!

I understand that congratulations are in order. Irene is a very fine girl, I am sure. Best wishes to you both, and much happiness. No doubt you have had snaps taken together. If you would send me one it would be very much appreciated.

It looks as though the war with Germany might be over any time. But you never can tell! When I was home in September we thought that it would be over by Christmas.

The Navy is still going strong. Cornwallis is as busy as can be, and training still continues.

Perhaps I shall be going to Ottawa next month to take a "Personnel Selection and Vocational Guidance" Course. It will mean hard work and three-hour exams, but I asked for it, so I can't complain.

Among the thousands here it is seldom that I see anyone from home. Howard Ryan is taking a Physical Training Course – it is a strenuous twelve weeks course. It looked like old times to see him refereeing a Wren Basketball game the other night.

Jackie Dawson is here also – and John Barrett. Before Christmas Jack James, who used to work in Trench's was on a course – he is a Lieutenant. Vincent Griffin is an Engineer Lieutenant stationed here. Do you remember him? He went through school in Kelowna from Grade 2 to Matric and was in the same class as Brian Bell, Janet Hay and Rene Jennens. He lived in Glenmore – and played the piano for Nancy Gale's choir.

Muriel Cunliffe is in Halifax – also Shirley Willits. Evelyn MacQueen is in the Naval Library here and Nancy Collett is a teletype operator in the office right next door to mine. How these Kelowna girls get around!

We can certainly be proud of our Mother. I teased her about making both the front and back page of the Courier!

It is quite an experience to spend a winter in Nova Scotia. It hasn't been nearly as cold as the two winters I spent in Ottawa, but the storms have been hectic. A storm blows up in no time at all and rages for two or three days. We wear sou' westers and rubber boots and do our best to keep our feet on the ground. In between storms there are periods of lovely, mild, almost warm weather.

And now 'tis time to turn in. It is hard to get enough sleep in the navy.

Please write and tell me more about your plans.

My best wishes to you both.

Frances

S.D. Treadgold
Kelowna, B.C.

March 14th 1945

Dear Bill-

Your letter received yesterday. Thanks. This is Jim's birthday and I have just written him, better late than never, but it is better never late. The weather is mild and like spring. Glad to hear you are busy. It seems best to keep busy. Dad seems to keep almost too busy. I think he is getting rid of the cold and then I believe he will be much better there for a long time. He is still thinking of going to Vancouver and may take Barry with him, but he doesn't see what he can do to help Bert and Grandpa out. They will have to fix up their own mess if there is one. We don't think Bert knows anything and then again Isobel won't leave, not her, unless she finds someone with a fortune. You have to have money to live and if she had wanted to work, she would have done so before this. We had a letter from Nell and nobody seems to know for sure so that is as far as it will get, but I may be wrong. I was going to write last night the lights went out for over an hour so we sat in the dark. I was just getting started - just this section of the town. Frances is a Lieutenant now. It was Automatic. I just had to put ink in my pen it does not seem to want to write.

Frances address for now is:

  St. F. Treadgold: W.R.E.N. Hardy House
  443 Daly Ave. Ottawa, Ont.

She says the course is a stiff one. I only had a note but expect a letter soon.

I have so little news for you and the cookies I hope to get off in a day or so.

Barry received your letter the other day. They are both full of beans and are playing outside quite a lot now. Last night I did not call them and they did not come in until almost 6:30 and supper over. What fun for a few minutes. He enjoyed his supper after that. I made them get ready for bed first. Next time they will be on time. I didn't spank them just told them there was no supper for them. Barry said he did not have a watch.

I am glad you and Irene are able to enjoy your 48 leave.

I see by the Province that Mr. and Mrs. Burr Sr. are divorced. Too bad he was such a drunkard.

There will be lots after this war is over. One wonders where it will all end sometimes.

I will be glad when it is warm enough to work in the garden.

Great Grampa has a birthday on the 2nd April. Alison's was 6th March, Vie 1st and Jack on the 10th April.

I sent the paper. Well Bill I must get to work, but will write again before long. Give my regards to Irene and write soon

    With love

        Mother

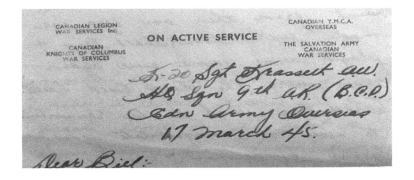

K-20. Sgt. Krasselt A.W.
HQ Sqn. 9 C.A.R. (B.C.D.)
Cdn. Army Overseas
17 March 1945

Many thanks Bill for your swell letter and snaps.
As you may already know we're now in Belgium and
hence the delay in mail.

Yours truly just returned from 8 days in London
so as you can see, we do get around a bit in
this Army.

When I opened your letter, I was sitting with Len
Roth and Carl Tostenson so of course I showed them
the snaps etc. Course you can imagine how the
conversation went from then on. Yes, we made every
basketball trip and played every game over again-
them were the days Bill.

Bill and the Kelowna Basketball team circa 1939

Both Carl and Len wish to be remembered to you and congratulate you on your engagement.

Yes, Bill, Irene looks very nice, but then She would have to be.

Where did all the family come from though!! And what in hell is the idea of your standing one step above Her in the picture and making her look so short!!

Well Bill since I last wrote to you much has happened. As I said before we're now in Belgium and what a treat it is for us. It's really a beautiful country and spotlessly clean. The people are grand and nearly "kill us with kindness". I have a swell room in a private home and it's just a "home away from home" to me. A guy can't do a thing for himself. No not even polish your boots. What a change from Itie land. We're located in quite a good size town at the moment, and although

I haven't been out at all myself, the boys are really having a time for themselves.

My leave to England was a big surprise and a very nice break. Needless-to-say my return was not what I had at one time contemplated, however I did have a fair time. One of my cousins had a few days off in which we went skating, dancing and took in several good films and plays. Should have got up to Scotland while there, but I'd done so much travelling that I was quite content to stop in one place for a day or two.

Well Bill I'll sign off now and hit the hay. I'm Orderly Joe tonight and 5 A.M. comes early in the morning.

Goodnight Chum—

Good luck and every best wish from a guy named—

no not Joe—but

    Krassy or Alban

                    Mar. 21 /45

                    Penticton, B.C.

Dear Bill:-

I am really ashamed of myself for saying we would be in Vancouver and not showing up and then taking so long to answer you. We could not make it when we said on account of the accident in the canyon which you no doubt heard of as Bob had to leave here and Elsie had to stay here to look after things. We arrived in Vancouver on the following Wednesday and left Friday night. The driver that went over in the canyon broke his leg three places but is coming along OK.

I haven't forgotten you by any means but we have bought a lot here and are preparing to build and I have been working on it every minute of spare time I get. It is down near the lake and is 60 by 161.5 ft. so I will have a lot of garden and lawn to look after. We are building a place 18x22 ft. on the back corner to live in and will have it for a garage and workshop later when we build a house. When you and Irene visit us there we hope you will spend a night with us.

I had today off and both worked clearing it up until dark so won't have any trouble sleeping to night. My foot is coming along alright but I have to be a little careful yet.

Hope you forgive us for not being there but the accident occurred Sat. morning and it was impossible to get away. <u>I don't like Van.</u> So come up here so I won't have to go through there to see you. With best regards to you and yours from both of us.

As ever,

John

Bell, J.H.

4 Anti Tank Regt.,

R.C.A. C.A.O.

23 Mar 45

Dear Bill -

Received a very pleasant surprise last week in the form of a letter with pictures from you. When I saw this large business-like envelope addressed to me, I thought the government had finally caught up with me, and once more I would have to dig deep & pay my overdue income tax - so it was quite a relief also.

Kidding aside Bill, I do appreciate your thoughtfulness. When you mentioned my note of congratulations to you both, I assure you it was sincere. You see, Irene & I are very close. We've had to stick together for a long time.*

She wrote me how you two met, and fell in love; also, of the many pleasant outings you've had, especially as regards sports. I think you'll find practically the whole Bell family goes in for sports of some sort or another.

I feel sure you will try to make Irene as happy as possible, and know you can do it.

As for myself I am at present in Belgium. Unfortunately, I didn't get into any big scraps in Italy, but—.

After attending talks by Montgomery, I really hope we shall be in for the final kill on German soil — which let's hope isn't too far distant.

We are now getting ready for our biggest moment.

Again, my sincerest good wishes to your future happiness.

Sincerely,

Harry B.

*Upon learning of his sister's engagement, Harry hired a private investigator to check out Bill, as he would have done had he not been away at war. Bill obviously 'made the grade'.

Harry Bell

Harry & Irene

S.D. Treadgold
Kelowna, B.C.
March 25 - 1945

Dear Bill-

Well Bill I don't know that I have much news but felt like getting off a line. Dad may be leaving for the coast on Wednesday the 28th. I think he will make up his mind before I mail this. It is difficult to get a sleeper, but he may go anyway and take Barry. If he doesn't get the sleeper, he will leave tomorrow he will take a rug and a small pillow and manage. There is not much fun travelling these days and then it is impossible to get a place to stay when you get there. They will stay with Jim, Violet very kindly asked them.

Frances passed her first part, there are two or more parts. She said all her class passed. One letter was quite interesting telling of the ones taking the course, all being officers I think, either Majors or St. Commanders and such and the examiners were all ex. officers too and she had to give a five- minute talk on Rehabilitation. She was very nervous but said she was still alive and she got through that too and then went and had her hair done and went to a show and enjoyed sitting on a soft seat and a good show. At Cornwallis the seats are all hard. She is getting a new uniform so she must expect to stay put for a while, and a new brief case and a steamer trunk so now she is broke for awhile.

Dad expects to stay over the weekend. I must do up the paper and get it off too. I expect I will be busy getting them off and then holding the fort. I hope they enjoy the change and I think they will. Dad has his new suit. I have not seen it, but he said it is nice and he may wear it, and Barry will wear his too. I am going to get him a pair of shoes tomorrow. They will get shabby. The crocuses are out plenty now and are very nice indeed.

Well chin up and drop a line when you have time.

I have so little news. Scotty Lore was back this week and he said Bert does not look very well although he was some better. I don't think he likes the look of things.

Monday noon

Well Bill, Dad will leave here all being well on Wed. the 28th C.N.R. which leaves at 10 to 5, he was lucky to get a cancelled sleeper. They are beginning to get excited

       With love

          Mother

                 S.D. Treadgold
                 Kelowna, B.C.

                 March 30 1945

Dear Bill –

Well here goes for a line even if I am tired. I was cleaning up my garden and it looks nice too, hundreds of crocuses out I am glad it is clean but it is tiring. I am wondering if Dad will be going to Victoria, he said he might but then he may not. He and Barry went off pretty smart, saying they were going to have a good time so I hope they enjoy the change.

Bill's Mother, Father and Barry

I had a letter from Frances tonight and she will be through her course now and stays there for a week and then goes to Halifax temporarily, she will be until the discharge system has been properly set up. There will be one large discharge centre on the East Coast and the West Coast with probably a couple of small ones in between. She has two more stripes put on her uniform with a green stripe between them being a special branch instead of executive. She says she is thinner. She has to report to H.M.C.S. Stadacona Halifax on the 9th of April. It is a very large base. 1200 WRENS there.

I had a letter tonight from Annie at Kitchener, 321 Frederick. She would like you to write her I am sure, as she asked for you. She expects Elmer home on leave late in the summer, she has not been well, fell down cellar but is better I think, so write her. I am almost too tired to write a decent letter. I am glad you and Irene are getting out some and hope you will be able to see Dad. I have not got the furnace on this week so have to keep better fires in the kitchen. I will send the Courier with this letter.

When Donna saw Barry in his suit, she said 'he looks like a man'. I had to smile. Miles and Donna were colouring eggs after supper, what a mess. Miles wanted to hide them in the garden. I told him it might rain and so it will, I think. That was why I wanted it all clean today.

I see by the Province Tommy Brydon has been in honoured with a medal and Don Poole too has been honoured so Kelowna has had a number. I saw by the paper a lot of English mail was bound (for Canada) when the plane took off.

When Dad left this time, he said, well you haven't a dog or chickens to feed this time. I think the first time in History. I think Dad feeding Kerry taught him a lesson. I smile every time I think of it. I let him do it and did he eat a lot. He was always thinking of feeding Kerry.

Miles' Bantam rooster lives here most of the time. I think he gets more to eat here and about a dozen cats come in the back yard. I think people must starve their animals.

It's nice today but a cool wind. Just going to get lunch and then go shopping. Write soon.

     With best wishes to Irene

       As ever Mother

          K-20. Sgt. Krasselt A.W.
          HQ Sqn. 9 C.A.R. (B.C.D.)
            Cdn. Army Overseas

                 4 April 45

Dear Oscar:

Many thanks for your swell letter of 4 March and the enclosed pictures. Must say Bill you do look rather "love sick" or something leaning against that tree. Better pick a bigger one next time. The "Gal Friend" does look very nice and of course that fishing scene looks very familiar. Them were the days eh kid? Guess I'll have to go fishing by myself in future as all you fellows have gone and got "hitched" on me. However as the song goes "I don't worry 'cause it makes no difference now". Ha Ha

Yes Bill Carl is still with us and so is Eric Waldron. Art Burtch had an accident in Italy and had his arm crushed by the recoil of a gun. He was evacuated to England and I haven't heard from him nor seen him since. Think he'll be okay though.

You speak about food Bill. Well, it varies with the times and places, and one gets very sick of it at times. However, that's to be expected. We do have separated messes at times, but usually eat together out under the stars, sun, rain or what have you. Believe it or not the wind was so strong today it took the marg off the bread as quick as one could spread it on. Some fun eh.

We just left the grandest billets we've had since we left home. I'll never forget the kindness and hospitality shown me by the family with whom I stayed. They were really swell.

We spent 14 hrs of Easter Sunday on the road so saw many an Easter parade. The weather wasn't very nice though, so wooden shoes and old hats came very much to the fore.

Must close now Bill and crawl into the tent for a few hours "fart sack drill".

Hoping that this finds you as well as it leaves me. Regards to your "Fair Lady" and same to everyone else I know.

Au revoir—Good luck

    Your chum

        Krass

S.D. Treadgold
Kelowna, B.C.

April 8th 45

Dear Bill –

Well, I am wondering where you are tonight. Dad and Barry are back. They could get a sleeper for Thursday night only so that seemed the best thing to do. They enjoyed the change and Dad saw a doctor about his nose so let's hope it will clean up now. Everybody in Vancouver seemed fine. Barry is full of beans.

I had a letter from Frances and she will be on her way to Halifax. She was in Montreal for Easter and enjoyed it. Frances' address for the time is

Lt. F.M. Treadgold
W.R.E.N.S
H.M.C.S. Stadacona
% F.M.O
Halifax N.S.

Mrs. Cattee and Louise were at Jim's from Saturday so they had a full house. The weather was rather cool and has been here too. Good Friday was the warmest day we have had.

Dad is here doing books; he was trimming up the trees today.

You may know that Jack has a lovely boat now. Mr. Grant that worked for Jones built one for himself. It's a very good boat, all finished but the seats and a few jobs also putting the engine in it, so he went away up Prince George way and could not take it as it would cost about $350 freight so Jack got it. I think perhaps Jim knew he was thinking of getting it, he never knew for sure until just a week ago. It is 20 ft long and about 7 wide so we will all be able to have a ride some time. I expect he will fit it up nicely.

Jack has been playing a lot so I expect perhaps he put his orchestra money to help pay for it - although I don't know what it cost. Miles will have a big time this summer.

The children go back to school tomorrow and I am not sorry. I have the paper ready for mailing. Dad says he has quite a lot of work in the shop seeing he was away for 10 days or almost.

Frances says she has got quite a lot thinner and I expect she will look better but I hope she does not get too thin.

Mr. Chapman told Dad he thinks perhaps Joyce is on her way home.

Houses are still scarce here. John who works for dad has to move this month but he can't find any-thing simply not a place, as bad as Vancouver.

Barry and Miles play ball now so watch my flowers this year. They have started already. I don't believe I told you Henry Burtel died on Easter Sunday suddenly, he will be missed.

Dad got Miles and Barry each a nice raincoat and Donna a new dress. That was the extent of his purchases.

The trains home have been late, K.V.R, going around by Spencer's Bridge. We will all be glad to have some warm weather.

Frances said Harry Webb and Alan Cameron are on their way overseas. She did not see them but they were in Ottawa last week.

Frances was down at Headquarter for experience this week.

The apricot trees are almost out in blossom, so when it gets warmer, they will all be out. Dad thinks it is as far ahead here as Vancouver this year, so it is late there.

The war news looks good, but they may hang out a long time. The towns and cities seem to be getting ready for Victory Day. Dad might get some work for that; I would not be surprised. Well Bill, write soon. I am afraid I was longer this time, I kept busy having everything to do, so will lay the table for breakfast. Give my regards to Irene. I must write her so will say good night.

    With my love

        Mother

Dear Bill

Thanks so much for the nice Easter card. I have quite a collection now. I must make more cookies soon and send on.

Well, I guess this is all for now

        Mother

Porter, E.A.
No. 15 "X' Depot,
RCAF, Kamloops, BC
April 11, 1945

Believe it or not, that's my signature at the end
of this letter!

Dear Bill,

I certainly enjoyed receiving your letter of March
26 and want to apologize for leaving it unanswered
so long. Rest assured that the D.R.O. you were
good enough to send me will take an honoured place
amongst my most treasured souvenirs by virtue of
all the friendly expressions of goodwill and kind-
liness which "the gang" endorsed thereon. Believe
me I was deeply touched and when I review the some-
what crazy sequence of days which followed each
other in hectic fashion during my altogether (damn?
I must be stunned!) all too brief stay at Patricia
Bay, I can assure you that many of the scenes
which now pass before my mind's eye are viewed
through a most closely akin to tear, even though
the numerous attendant violent displays of temper
on the part of a certain little belligerent flight
lieutenant must have given the casual onlooker an
impression that all h--l had broken loose!

"The Gang" from Pat Bay

Y/O Johnson no doubt expressed it very aptly when
he described me as sometimes getting so mad, I
jumped up once and came down twice and threw my
keys in two different directions at once! However,
there were many compensations for all the grief
and general wailing and weeping and explosive
rhetoric which seemed to dominate the Bay Masters'
existence during those never - to - be forgotten
months of 1944. If, as perchance sometimes happened, I was feeling exceedingly blue and craved a
tonic for my harried soul, I had only to step into
the outer office and take a quick peep at you, my
dear Willie, immersed in reams of paper and surrounded by hordes of sweating, swearing, snarling,
raving human beings to be immediately transported
from the depths of despondency to the heights of
hilarious bliss! Not that I took a sadistic delight
in viewing your trials and tribulations, but the
sight of you - standing steadfast and resolute
amidst a setting mass of turbulent humanity with

that indescribable look of resignation and silent suffering stamped upon your classic feature, and exhibiting a masterly restraint such as I have never witnessed before or hope to see again, was often too much my distorted sense of humour and I would retire into my den positively exploding with suppressed mirth.

After this, the only thing required to fill my cup of joy to overflowing was to have Sgt. Shillington, wearing that harried look of distraction (which seems to be the Pat Bay hallmark of distinction insofar as Accounts personnel are concerned!) come raging into my office, snorting fire and brimstone, and breathing dire threats against all the dirty so-and-so's who insisted on pestering him with all sorts of weird and wonderful questions regarding their pay accounts! Ha! Ha! Ha!

Those were the good old days when we were all stunned in a different way! All I seem to do is sit and gaze aimlessly into space whilst the slow sonorous seconds beat out the measured march of time across this vast vale of desolate denuded dunes studded with sandy sterility! And just imagine Willie this is just one hundred miles from Utopia! Ah! Well, probably I am a little bitter about the whole thing and shouldn't be taken too seriously, but candidly Willie, I do believe this immediate locality is situated very far back, way, way back in the rear-most portion of the world's anatomy, if you get what I mean! However, I do know your beloved Kelowna is everything you claim for it and shall certainly visit there before I leave this desert wilderness, which sounds paradoxical, but only applies to the Kamloops area.

Kind regards to all the gang not to mention a certain someone!

    E.A. Porter

                                  S.D. Treadgold

                                  Kelowna, B.C.

                            April 18th, 1945

Dear Bill –

Well here it is Wednesday again, just 9 a.m. I intended writing last night but time went quickly and I did not get at it. The weather is just a little warmer and we are all fine, I received your letter yesterday and glad you are fine.

Frances arrived at her new station and she is not at "Stadacona" but a short distance away, instead it is H.M.C.S. "Peregrine". She would just as soon be there as it is not so huge. She said the weather is nice and warm. It was a short letter so I expect another soon.

Like you we are all feeling sorry to lose a man like the late President. I think everyone sort of feels a personal loss. It is to be hoped the new man will be a good man. They are very close to us. The war with Japan may take a time and I think all peoples would like a world of Peace. They surely have put Germany under and I suppose it had to be for they have been such beasts. I can't understand it. I think it is beyond most people. It is a good thing we are not under them.

I want to go up town this morning. Barry and Donna took their lunch today. They like to sometimes.

They have lunch kits and think it fine. They both look very well and I think Donna is growing most now.

I have been wondering if Jim will be getting off as by the radio Vancouver is short of labor, we will soon know, I guess.

Dad was sorry to have not seen you and I think would have stayed over if he had heard from you, but as you know Jim was full up with the Cattees being there and Dad did not want to put people out. They were very good to him and then again sleepers are so hard to get on short notice and that was the only night and he booked it a week before, and then too he is busy here.

I think his nose is getting better. I expect he had too many head massages, the oil is what they said caused it, but he never uses oil. I expect the Barber did, when he rubbed his head, so now that is out and he has to shampoo more, quite often. The blood vessel running down to the nose is supposed to be the cause. So, he is feeling better since his teeth are right, he feels quite natural now, thank goodness. I sent you the paper on Monday and I will enclose a letter from overseas. Mr. Chapman told me David was married, last Xmas Eve to a girl in Rhodesia. He said it seemed to be quite a nice wedding and asked me to go and see Mrs. Chapman and see the pictures. I believe he is going to England. The first time in five years. I heard Mr. Bob Gordon say his boy Bill is quite English by what Jack Gordon said after seeing him in England. His manners etc. quite an Englishman. He is supposed to be here now. I also hear that perhaps Howard Williams may be coming home, not sure, he is in England for treatment to his eyes and I believe Tim Armstrong is coming home after an illness. So, they come and go.

Well Bill I must get busy if I am going up town. Write soon. Give my love to Irene.

With love from us all,

        As ever,

              Mother.

Excuse the scribble always in a hurry

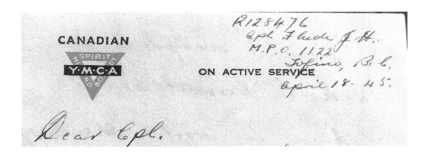

                Cpl Flude, J.H.

                April 18/45

Dear Cpl.

I am slow at writing. I should have let you know before that I found my ring. Before I left I told the S.P.s to notify you in case someone found it. Well I saved them the trouble.

When I was packing my blankets in my kit bag it must have come off. I was sure glad.

Maybe you have heard that A.T. trick they pulled on me, I was sure peeved.

They sent one of the lads from this point when I got to Tofino and kept me here. They did it after I was Posted.

Never mind, I hope this little quarrel will soon be over and everybody is back to normal again. I have to write the boys at Pat Bay so they will get a laugh out of it.

Now I must thank you many times for your kindness and I hope you will overlook me not writing sooner and letting you know.

Hoping you are quite well.

> Yours sincerely
>
> Harry

> S.D. Treadgold
> Kelowna, B.C.
>
> April 23rd 1945

Dear Bill -

Well here almost another week has gone and the weather is a little warmer with showers today, which is good for my flowers. The garden is quite nice now what a change in a week.

I had a letter from Frances yesterday and one from you today. Frances is fine and busy as usual; she has to take the bus to work at Stadacona but she says it is better staying where it is not quite so crowded. She was talking to Colin Carruthers;

he looks very well. You and Irene manage to get around, and have a fair time, which is nice.

I really have very little news. Dad is quite busy as usual. The children are sleeping on the veranda now in the glassed part. They both look very well. Donna can ride Wilma's bike, she has more nerve than she had, she says you are still her sweet heart, she is full of fun.

I have not got these cookies off yet. I will get around to it sometime I hope.

It took 8 days for Frances' letter to come. I wonder if the censor air mail holds them up for they seem to be censored. I have been wondering when Jim will be coming this way.

So they are in Berlin now. It may take them a time to clean up and then again it may not be long. I think Matthew Halton gives the best description of the real war. He seems to see war in its real senses. [Matthew Halton was a Canadian TV journalist, most famous as a foreign correspondent for the CBC during WWII -Wikipedia]

Scotty Lore is in Vernon now and he comes home quite often. He says there is to be a permanent camp there they are painting and fixing it up I think.

I sent the paper on Monday. The weeks seem to fly. I am glad it is the good summer coming, we get tired of the cool weather.

The Canadians are getting a taste of Germany now. They will be glad when it is over.

I still have some garden to plant so I must get energetic and finish up.

I have so little news but this will let you know we are fine. Write soon.

With heaps of love, From us all

Hope Irene is feeling fit again.

      As ever

          Mother

                  S.D. Treadgold
                  Kelowna, B.C.

                  May 10th 45

Dear Bill –

You will be wondering what has happened to me. I have been busy one way and another so just kept thinking. Many thanks for the candy Bill. I am enjoying one when I feel like it.

I had a letter from Jim so I expect you saw Wilma. I do hope she makes the grade this time.

Harold got back yesterday and he seemed to think she was fairly good.

Dad has been quite busy. I was up this afternoon to help get straight. I have not been up for a long time and it had almost got beyond Dad. Between customers and pictures etc. he doesn't get time to keep straight and he has been making new holders for his wall paper, which these days is quite a business as the stock is in and out all the time. The kids have just gone to bed. They were at the shop with me and I had a lunch for them so they enjoy that.

I hope Irene is better. I must drop her a line, between getting Wilma ready and worry I felt, feel I could not write a decent letter.

Dexter Pettigrew was married today. I sent last week's paper to Vancouver hope you saw it. I will send this week's to you tomorrow and I will enclose a letter from Over Seas.

Dad was just telling me that John, the man who works for him had a wire to say his brother's wife (war bride) wired she is on her way from England and he has to get out of his house, had notice months ago and no place to go, he is building or making over a shack, just started and it is not big enough for his two children and her one. They don't know what they will do. I say they should stay in the house for awhile. The owners had lawyer write him and if they put him out it will cost him $40. I hear there are at least 30 families have to move. It seems serious here I don't know what the returning men will do, have to double up I suppose. Some of these war brides won't think it so wonderful, but they may be at home moving around, after all the bombing.

There are lots of homes going up everywhere, such a change. I think John is going to get the Elks to help shingle. I saw Jack's boat and it is very nice indeed, it will be one of the nicest on the lake but not the largest, but it is quite roomy and good. Mr. Jones is putting the engine in and then there is a little finishing such as seats, but not a lot. I guess he will make it pretty nice.

Colin MacLean is missing. Stuart Webster wounded - I don't know how serious. Well Bill excuse the delay, I didn't forget you for a minute and again many thanks for the candy. Don't spend your money on me but I do appreciate them all the same.

My garden is at its best now - very nice.

So with lots of love from us all,

As ever

Mother

V.E. Day was very quiet here. They did have a service at the park. I dressed the children nicely and Dad decorated their bicycles so went up alone and enjoyed it.

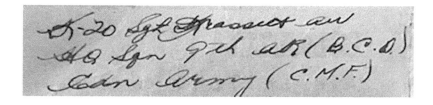

K-20. Sgt. Krasselt A.W.
HQ Sqn. 9 CAR (BCD)
Cdn. Army Overseas

17 May 45

Dear Bill:-

Here I am at last with a few lines in answer to your ever welcome letter of 23 April which I received a few days ago.

Well Bill its all over now—at least in these parts— and how the civies are whooping it up. They've been parading, dancing etc. for over a week now and are still going strong. It certainly must be a big relief for them and they're sure letting off the steam. Strange as it may seem the boys took it all very matter of a fact. We didn't as much as get an hour off and personally I've been as busy or busier than we were when in action. However, it can't go on for ever now at least we hope not. Sure would like to be home for Regatta but if I make it for Xmas I'll be lucky I think. 'Course I could be home for 30 days sooner if I volunteered for the Far East. I'd do that too if it wasn't for Mother and Dad. However as neither of them have been very well I think I'd better be home when I get the chance and cause no further worry.

Just in case you think I'm still in Italy Bill such is not the case. We've been over here in Belgium and Holland since the early part of the year. It's sure a swell change for us too after "Itie land".

Had a couple of swell dances in the town we were stationed in last week and expect to go back tomorrow night for another 'go'. 'Course it's always my luck to end up with a gal that can't speak a word of English, but as the song goes "It makes no difference now"

Well Bill I seem to have shot my wad for this time so will sign off.

Hoping that this finds you as well as it leaves me, this is, as ever,

Your chum

Krassy

S.D. Treadgold
Kelowna, B.C.

May 17th 1945

Dear Bill –

Your letter received Bill. Pleased to hear Irene is on the well list again. I had a letter from Frances yesterday and she saw little of the rioting. She was walking home after attending the service with another WREN Officer and remarked how quiet and everything seemed to be. Had they walked through the downtown section it would have been a different story. She says it could have been avoided to a certain extent. The minute Victory was declared everything was closed up tight. The stores, restaurants, theatres. Nothing was planned to celebrate the day so there was absolutely nothing to do. [The Halifax VE-Day riots, 7-8 May 1945 in Halifax began as a celebration of the WW 2 Victory. It rapidly evolved into a rampage by several thousand servicemen, merchant seamen and civilians, who looted the City of Halifax.] The navy got the blame but all services and civilians did their share in full force. That was about all she said. I saw a letter written in The Vancouver addressing this by a Halifax WREN to her father and it was much the same, only much fuller. It was pretty bad, I guess.[xxiv]

I have not heard of Wilma yet, only from Jim to say she was not too bad and the doctor was back. I'm sure we'll be getting a letter one of these days. We are wondering if Jim will be getting off. It looks like Violet may have to stay in Penticton for awhile – their house will be empty

some time - as the man (renter?) is building but houses are as bad or worse. I don't know what all the return people will do. The weather has been raining lately and not too warm. This is Thursday afternoon. I will get this off today. I expect to go uptown, will send the paper tomorrow.

So, you and Irene hope to be married in October. You will have something to look forward to and plan for. The time seems to go so quickly and I expect you will have lots to think about. All these things seem to come in time. There seems to be a large fruit crop again this year. Barry and Donna are fine and growing like weeds. I have very little news. I have been house cleaning and getting things in order. This is a big place to keep in good shape so there is very little idle time. Thank yourself and Irene for the nice Mother's Day card; yours was different. They were all very nice and much appreciated. Sunday afternoon Dad and I drove to Eldorado Arms. Dad had to see the owner so we had tea with them. It was a nice afternoon. We happened to run into Mrs. Walter Trump. She was visiting Mr. Wm Lloyd Jones for a few days and her boy at Oliver. Arthur Lloyd Jones is in Peregrine, where Frances is, she sees him often, he is on Shore Patrol. Dad has a crew but he is still very busy and they are busy in the store too. The crew keep him busy. Well Bill I think I will go uptown, write soon.

With heaps of love to you both,

From us all

As ever Mother

S.D. Treadgold
Ailsa Lodge
1020 Melville St.
Vancouver, B.C.

May 25th

Dear Bill –

Well Bill you will no doubt be surprised to see
where I am today, but I expect to leave tomorrow
with Jim for home. Wednesday morning Violet phoned
Dad from Penticton and said Wilma would not take
the treatments and the doctor did not know what
to do, so I caught the C.N.R. that night got here
yesterday morning, got my room and went straight
to the hospital phoned the doctor and have things
straightened out for the time being. Wilma was
not so good. I thought she had lost some and the
doctor said she simply went to pieces when he
tried to force her. It seems she remembers not
the last treatments but ones before and she gets
so nervous, however I talked to her and I think
she will now. He will give her something if she
refuses and she will get her first treatment tomorrow. She would have had one today but the nurses
were full up for the day. He says after the first
two she won't mind. I am going home and come back
in a couple of weeks or so. I do hope she shows
improvement and that it will be lasting. It is so
hard to say. If you are in town next week go and
see her and take her some oranges or juice (apple)
or grape or something. I will give you the cash. I
won't forget and she likes popcorn and it doesn't
hurt her. She misses the good food at home. She was
looking so well and seemed bright. Today I thought
her some better than yesterday. I would stay as I

can do, but still, I will get so lonely here alone and nothing to do. The time will seem so long and I must think of myself too. I think and hope they will look after her.

The kids were fine. Jim and I went and called on Mrs. Bell [Irene's mother] after supper Th. night. I was pleased to meet her and the family and then we called Grandpa and I saw the Ludlows yesterday so we have been busy. If all is well tomorrow we will leave after lunch for home. Jim and I and may stay off somewhere and finish Sunday. I will try and let you know if I am coming a little later. The doctor says she might come out of it - you just can't tell. I didn't wear my ring today and she asked me where it was, so she sees things. I don't expect to see her tomorrow as she will have had a treatment, but will ask for her.

I will drop Frances a line now to while away the time. I don't sleep very well and don't like being alone, but I won't give in if I can help it. I will say good night now.

    With love to you both

      Mother

Sat. a lovely morning and I think I will be going home today - if not I will write tomorrow.

R.144505

L.A.C. "Gil" K.D.

R.C.A.F. Overseas

June 2, 1945

Dear Bill,

This is the promised letter, and it's about time I wrote to you too. Anyway, after you read it, I'm sure you'll agree that I've done some travelling in less than two months. Here goes.

After leaving Halifax on the 14th and staying on the ocean for seven glorious days we finally landed in Greenock Scotland, because of the size of the ship "Aquitania"[xxv] travelling all day and nite of the 22nd of April that is!

We arrived at No.3 P.R.O. Bournemouth staying there three days for documentation and further selection on this type of work, thence to Kenley still in Southern England but in the County of Surrey, only a few miles from London. There was another short stay for our Armament training was to be at Patwich (Surrey). We had our longest stay there, departing on the 15th of May to Hornchurch to board our L.S.T. boat this taking us to Ostend Belgium travelling through Antwerp, crossing the border into Holland and sleeping out that nite by the roadside, starting off early next morning for Nijmegan Holland to bed down for the nite. Rising early next morning and getting off again (all travelling has been trucks) shortly after we left, we came into the town of Arnhem, quite a few good Canadians lost their lives there on and around the 19th of Sept, last arriving late that evening at a German airfield situated in the county of Twente Holland just another few days and stop over before proceeding to the camp well into Germany.

There's the restriction on telling just where but by the end of this month these will be lifted. We're not far from the Belsen Con. Camp[xxvi] and it's really true what the News Reels reveal and also the Papers because I've seen evidence right around here, kids walking along the roads with nowhere to go because their folks have all been burned or otherwise starved to death, one old man came into camp today and showed us the scars from the beatings, broken nose, busted fingers, spiked hands and many other tales. The S.S. men and women are on review in the town close by and we've all had the opportunity to watch these rats parading, they're sullen and don't seem to know how long they've got to live, the women are really a tough lot and the personal records should be ready soon for we guys to Seal. I'll keep in touch with you and give you a good description of them. Out of forty men in prison there's only eleven that can parade because they're stowing them so I'm told, and they really look it too! Are you getting tired?

The other day I had the opportunity of seeing all of Hanover, this is sure bombed out but nothing in comparison with Bremen or Berlin so I'm led to believe. If that's so, nothing is left of those cities. Honest Bill it's been travel, travel all these few days but I'd not miss this for anything, it's really different from the Humding of the W.A.C. [Western Air Command][xxvii] rules. We've got a softball diamond layed out & a volley ball court & tomorrow they start their league. Provinces are to be the representatives. B.C. is very strong! Ha! Ha! "So is Quebec!" Just broke my arm.

Enjoyed a show "Moonlight and Cactus"[xxviii] a very good attempt on the Y.M.C.A's part. Also, a Cactus was set up and the first beer arrived last week, German made. Mail is finally catching up to me and I'm trying to write to each and everyone in turn. I've written several letters to Pat Bay folk, Aileen Bishop and the 122 gang, also a chap in 8 BR. Maybe you've heard about me from one of these people. No?

The weather has been real wonderful all along making the trip more enjoyable too.

Well Bill may be by the time you secure this letter I'll be many miles from this spot, for I've still got some "more travelling" to do. Oh yes! I enjoyed VE Day in Kelling Kent and also London for I was in on several occasions. This part of the country is really beautiful.

I'll leave you now and sure hope to hear from you soon and good luck to you in your future and may your health be at its peak. Remember me to the swell gang again. Write soon

Sincerely

    "Gil"

        Auf Weiderstein

S.D. Treadgold

Kelowna, B.C.

June 5th / 45

Dear Bill –

I received your letter today and sorry to hear you did not think Wilma very good, she seems so funny and hard to understand. I had a letter from her yesterday written on May 31st and it was such a nice letter nothing wrong with it. It must have been one of her good moments, she also wrote a page to Barry and Donna and one to Harold, but mine was four pages. Isobel had called and she seemed pleased to see her and she wished me many happy returns of my birthday. I do wish she would get over this terrible thing and give us all a rest of thought. I don't know just what I will do yet. I may hear from the doctor.

Jim went to Penticton and Vie and Trudy came up with him so we are a family now for a week or two. The weather was nice today but it started to rain about five and has been raining since.

Miles went into hospital last night to have his tonsils out today.

I think he is fine. He had a 'special' today and was asleep part of the day. He may be home tomorrow or the next day. Jim took Alison to hospital tonight and was going in to see Wally Sexsmith who was badly burned some time ago. He seems to be coming along slowly.

Dad went up to the shop for awhile tonight. Jim has been helping too since he is back. I have been thinking of making cookies again and may soon. Frances is fine and busy. She says there are only two in Halifax now of her lot. She is not at all sure where she will be and likely they will be busy after the election. I sent you two papers today. The children are fine and growing fast. When I go to Vancouver, I will let you know. There is lots to do here with so many around but we get through. When I was in Vancouver Donna got on her knees and washed the kitchen floor on a rubber mat 'like Granny does it'. Imagine her small hands. She cut fresh flowers for the house and washed hers and Barry's handkerchiefs. She did these so well I wondered who had washed them. What a girl! She is growing more than Barry.

I may add to this a line if I get a letter in the morning. The house seems cool tonight, it is the rain.

I will enclose a letter from England.

Wed. morn. - did not get any mail this a.m. Vie will mail this for me. Give my love to Irene. I will enclose some cash to pay for Wilma's eats another time. This letter seems full enough with the added English letter. I hope you are feeling your best, with lots of love from all of us.

As ever

Mother

S.D. Treadgold
Ailsa Lodge
1020 Melville St.
Vancouver, B.C.

June 10 1945

Dear Bill-

Just thought I would drop you a line and let you know I am here. Arrived this A.M. Mad. Poole and her little girl were on the train and are staying at the Devonshire for 8 days and then going to some Island for a few days. It will be in sticks but different-some place where they the "Cunninghams" or in-laws have bought a thousand acres and turning into a resort. It looks like rain.

They were all fine at home. Vie and Trudy are there so we were a houseful. Jim is keeping busy in the shop and will I guess for awhile at least.

It is not warm. At home I think it really is warmer. The children have been bathing and fishing. They will take some watching this summer. Barry is almost big enough to be on his own. They seem so big after Trudy. She is a wise little mite. I will add to this after I have been to Hospital to see what is trump.

Monday-

I saw the Dr. today and Wilma is some better. I am taking her out tomorrow at 2:30 and take her back before 8 p.m. She seemed quite a little better today but it is hard to say. I expect to be here for this week and take Wilma out in the afternoon and as the week goes on, we will see. I will try and drop you a line later.

I am trying to get a line off to Dad now and go to the Post Office.

So with all my love,

Mother

Sunday 5:30 p.m.

Dear Bill-

Just a line Bill to let you know we are fine and almost on our way. This a.m. when Wilma woke she was fine. O.K. and today just fine. We got up around nine or after, dressed, packed. Checked out and went to the Georgia for breakfast. Then went to the Ludlows, had a little lunch. Quite nice and then after four Aunt Millie and Bill took us to the Ailsa for suit cases and we got tickets - and all fixed up and then we left them. Wilma was hungry and had a lovely hot supper she enjoyed. Here we are at the C.P.R. Station all ready to get on the train at 7:45. Early but still we will put in the time. It has been a good day really. I thought I would like to let you know last night she was much too tired, after 5 weeks it's too much to expect. Today not one bit nasty, so let's hope this is the turning point. I just thought I would like to let you know. I am writing this on my knee in the station after getting the paper and envelope at a news stand. I am glad to sort of get everything off so easily. It is wonderful how these things work to the good. So it is of no use to worry.

I enjoyed your visit so much and so glad to see you. I hope you enjoyed your day as it is warm here. I met one of the Goslison Boys and he asked for you. I really believe Wilma is so much better it will just take time to get 100% we hope. She looks tired at times. Well Bill I will write from home. Have a good rest and don't overdo it as it doesn't pay. Hoping to see you again when we will all be O.K. in the near future. Write soon

As ever - Mother

With regards to Irene and I hope her eyes are better. What a scribble.

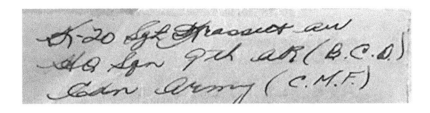

K-20 Sgt Krasselt AW
HQ Sqn 9 CAR (BCD)
Cdn Army Overseas.

19 June 45

Dear Bill:

Many thanks for your very welcome letter of 29 May which I received a few days ago. Glad to hear that someone else has trouble keeping up with the necessary letter writing. I've never been so far behind in my life, and just can't seem to settle down to it anymore. Once I get home, I'm afraid I'll never write another letter.

No Bill I won't be back to Canada on the first draft or any draft for that matter. We single men don't make out so well on this point system. Won't go into details on the matter, as I guess you've heard all about it. At the moment the drafts consist of CFEF men. Then the men with points ranging from 150 upwards. This will go on 'till August. After that Units will start going home as such. Of course units of the First Air will be first, then 2ⁿᵈ, 3ʳᵈ, 5ᵗʰ and 4ᵗʰ. How long all this will take is a big question, however we hope that the BCDs [B.C. Dragoons]) will make it back in time for Xmas. Carl Tostenson, Len Roth, Les Hungle and several others are going to the CFEF [Canadian Far

WENDY HAMILTON & CATHERINE PAVLIK

East Force], so will be going home on their 30 day leave soon. Then it will be the Pacific for them.

Very nice of you to ask me to be your best man Bill. As you know however its very hard to plan anything in the Army, and at the moment it looks as though we won't be home in time. However, I'll keep it in mind Bill and hope for the best.

So Dex Pettigrew and Doreen Noble have up and done it eh. I know for sure that I'll be the only single guy in town now. Guess you'd better "hand me down my walking cane".

Have been having a lot of trouble with my teeth lately in fact for the past couple of weeks they've nearly driven me crazy. Think I've finally got them beat now though.

Had a mess dance last week and expect another on Thursday. Just trying to make up my mind whether or not to make a date with one of these "cheese headed bags" or go stag. Some of these people are worse than the "wops". All they seem to know is to bum you for everything you got. They seem to think that a "Canadases Saldate" is a walking grocery store or something.

Was on POW escort duty for a couple of weeks and watched no less than 140 thousand 'Jerries' plodding their weary way home on foot. No, I didn't envy their getting home before me, as I wouldn't fancy getting there on my two flat feet, dragging my worldly belongings behind me in anything from baby carriages to home made carts. It was really quite a sight.

The weather here is quite fine but it doesn't seem to get very hot. Sure could go for some real O.K. heat. However, I guess I'll get some next year.

Will sign off now Bill and drop you a line again soon.

Au revoir, with all best wishes from

    Your chum

        Krass.

              J.S. Treadgold
              July 45

Dear Bill:-

Just a short note to say Hello and let you in on one or two things. We got back fine, but won't be in our house till the 15th of August, but we are getting by fine. I have been working in the shop and they have kept me very busy, from Book work to slinging a little paint. I have tried to clean the place up a bit but don't know if I'll come out on top or not.

Dad, Jack and I have been talking things over lately and we are coming to the conclusion that we will build a store next to the shop as soon as possible. I have written 4 firms at the coast to see when stocks of sporting goods and other lines will be available. If enough stock is available soon I may take space in the shop in order to get an oar in so as to keep others from starting-up as there is a little talk around. We will build as soon as a permit is available and there is the stumbling block, so I wondered if you could get a permit easier than we could, being in the Forces. Engine around a little and if you think so I will send you the lot number and plan. I think they would issue you one quickly. I intend to take out a Sporting Goods city licence soon and will put it in both our names, it may even be better for you to apply for that but we will see soon.

It will take time to get in a stock and work up a business but there's no harm in trying, and I think there's a good opening here. I won't need to lose any time as I can work in the shop or paint if things are slow starting. I would like to have things going fair by the time you are discharged so we would have a little hole here for you.

I expect that between Dad and Mr. Cattee we can finance a building and I can go a ways in regards to a stock and your 10,000 will come in handy. Any how that is the end to which I am working, there should be plenty between the three of us, I hope to keep the Sporting Goods Store separate providing it will carry itself.

Let me know what you think Bill and what ideas you have on the subject.

I am setting up my tools to make up a stock of plugs for myself as I sold most the ones I made last winter, they should make a good side line, something to do in spare time or may even be worked to something good.

I may get you to contact some of the wholesalers I have contacted in order to hustle things on a bit. The uniform should work pretty good there, I will let you know what to do. I have just written in to Marshal-Wells, Mc & Mc, Lipsetts and McKenzie

White & Dunsmuir on bicycles. I have personally contacted them all before so hope some of them can act, but it may be too soon to expect much in the way of stocks.

Joe Spurrier is selling out to Robin Kendall, he is in the store now but is not taking over till the first of the year. It will make an even footing to start off there or almost.

Say hello to Irene, I hope she is fine. Wilma seems better but has a ways to go yet.

All for now, write soon

Jim

J.S. Treadgold
Sunny Okanagan - and How!

July 10/45

Dear Bill:-

Well its hot as hell here this week, I have felt it some, but am getting used to it now, or hope I am.

Got your letter last week and was glad to hear from you, hope that you can let me know, soon, the score on the building permit, I have made other enquiries and I doubt too if you can get a permit until you are discharged, but we will work on it by hook or by crook. I would like to get the permit (and then) am free to go ahead if things plan out as expected. I have had word back from some of the wholesalers at the coast and some are very anxious to help out, Marshal-Wells in particular would like to back me up and they handle the Spalding line which is a very good one, they are sending a man in this week to see me and talk over plans. They think I should handle other lines as well such as "good quality gifts", which may be O.K. - we shall see.

I may be held up some time for a building permit but can use half the shop to get started and it may pay me to do this as to get an oar in would count.

I have a couple of jobs for you to do if you will. 1st is to write Uncle "Wilf" as you know him better than me. Ask him how the supply of sporting goods is especially his lines - fishing tackle etc., tell him our plans, and ask him to send me on an Alcock's Catalogue (I guess it's Alcock, Laight & Westwood A.L. & W.) and any other Catalogues in that line and if they have a traveller in this district have him look me up next time he is in this vicinity. "String him a line anyway."

2nd Next time you are in Vancouver call in to the C.C.M. wholesale at 1010 Homes St. (about 2 blocks East of Granville) "Canadian Cycle and Motor Co: Offices and Warehouse". And I believe they close at 12 on Saturday, so govern yourself accordingly. Ask them if it would be possible to buy direct from them, - "repair parts" as I don't want to get them off the C.C.M. agents here. I don't expect one could get the agency for Bicycles and accessories as there are 2 or 3 agents here now, but feel them out on this line, and let me know what they have to say. I would at least like to get parts. Also try and get a parts catalogue, or have them send one up here. They may not like to say no to a party in the Services, so see what you can do.

This is all for now, excuse the writing as I am in bed, and that's not the best place to write so

The best for now

Jim

Write soon.

Porter, E.A.
Ava Lodge
Pigeon Lake, Ontario

July 29, 1945

Hello Bill

Well here we are just about at the end of our all too short vacation. Just a few more days before I'll be on that old rattle trap heading west and I really hate the very thought of it. Any other year wasn't too bad but this year it's terrific. But I guess there is very little I can do about it.

Well Willie, our wedding went off in fine style. A little rushed but otherwise perfect. Flo did marvelous as far as gifts were concerned and right here is where I want to be. Thank you and Irene for your kindness to us. I was truly thrilled when I received your card and gift. Words just failed me and I am very proud to have such a true friend. I'll never forget that Bill.

I also want to thank you and the gang for the telegram. These things will cling to our memory always for I bought Flo an album to paste all the cards and telegrams in.

Well Bill this isn't very long so I hope you'll excuse me. I'll relate all happenings to you upon return. So in the meantime give my regards to Irene and the gang.

As Ever

    Your friend

        Ernie

The Royal Bank of Canada
Supervisor's Department
Vancouver, B.C.

August 3, 1945

R 143019 Cpl. Treadgold, W.O.,
R.C.A.F. Station,
Patricia Bay, B.C.

Dear Mr. Treadgold:-

    With reference to your letter of August 2nd, the bank's plan for re-establishment of its men on military service assures you of a salary upon your return which obviates the necessity of your obtaining our permission to marry.

    May we take this opportunity of wishing you all happiness.

Yours truly,

Staff Officer

S.D. Treadgold
Kelowna, B.C.

Aug. 5, 1945

Dear Bill-

Well Bill it was nice to hear you this noon. We are all fine. We were all just a little surprised when your telegram arrived. When Jim handed it to me with a smile, I wondered what if it was a school telegram which I receive sometimes these days. I was going to send the couriers just then and it too went out of my head, so I sent them the next day. The Regatta was a great success. The best yet they say. Jack was so busy for the last while. Was in the shop very little for a week. I believe they took in over 13 thousand dollars. Jack seems to be a good manager and gets things done. He has been working with Mr. Broad over the regatta. I will let him reserve your room. I expect he will do it in the morning. I could not get him to stay, he may be out in the boat, needs a rest. He was going to Vancouver but changed his mind, he tried to get a room at the Georgia but couldn't just tried. I expect he has work to do and is tired. I think he intended to go down before Alison and Miles get back. Well I have been very busy. Jim Palframan left on Tuesday, may be back later, he is in Vancouver but we have not heard from him yet.

Opening Ceremony Kelowna Regatta

The family setting out on the boat for a day at the Kelowna Regatta

On Wednesday Vie and her sister and husband and Annie Treadgold all arrived for the Regatta and left Friday afternoon so it means quite a lot to put up, but they enjoyed their stay. They were out in the boat with Jim.

Jim has just come in from Penticton, he and Vie went down this morning. Wilma is better, thank goodness. Last week she was quite a lot better. She is working and more interested so perhaps she will make it this time. We surely hope so. I will see about a sleeper for your return or Dad will tomorrow so will add to this letter later and will also get the things ready to take to Vancouver. We will both be very busy and may go down about Wednesday and come back on Sunday. Dad has a little business there but has to get back in time to do work for the Stampede. He will surely be busy. Jim will be moving as the people are getting out on the 16th Violet said yesterday you could stay at their house, so I guess you won't be stuck. It is very difficult to get rooms everywhere but I thought if anybody could get in at the Royal Anne, Jack could.

I must write Frances. We will get Monteith address tomorrow.

Bedford Magazine Explosion – "a conflagration resulting in a series of explosions July 18-19, 1945, in Bedford Nova Scotia[xxix]

Frances said she would not care to go through The Explosion again – her room was blown and badly shaken, some things broken but the window was open so not broken and sash blown in. Her shade was blown off the lamp. The 4 a.m. blast was the worst and by that time everybody had the jitters she said. Everything was boarded up with lumber.

The kids are fine and all the questions they asked when I told them you were going to be married and about Irene too. They are full of beans and growing.

It was very warm today. Dad and I went to the
country to get fresh eggs and peaches. I will
add more tomorrow and let me know what you want
for now.

Give our love to Irene

With our love

Mother

Monday noon Jack got the hotel reservation this
morning and the wire for berth from Sicamous to
Vancouver has been sent. Will know shortly I
expect. I guess this is all for now. Will put this
in the mail.

With love to you both,

Mother

Address updates:

Lieut. F. Treadgold

W.R.C.N.S
H.M.C.S.
Peregrine
Halifax, Nova Scotia

Mrs. J. Heberle

7 Watford St
Toronto
Ontario

R-479 S-1

Flight Sarg. Monteith
R.C.A.F.
Coal Harbor, B.C

R142602 Sgt Fitzgerald J.J.
Comox M PO 1121 BC
6th August 1945

Dear Bill,

You young varmint. But my heartiest congratulations boy. I surely am pleased to hear the big news Bill and I can only wish most sincerely that you have a very happy and long life and a helluva lot of little troubles. About eight or ten of them would be a good start. The old world could do with a lot of Treadgolds after this mess has been cleaned up. I mean that young fellow so don't you go getting any notions of having one of these modern families of one or two off springs. Not at your age. With me it is a slightly different proposition and you will have almost twenty years start on me. Yes I have finally met the one I have been looking for and we have been engaged for a couple of months. We are hoping to get married early in December. Perhaps sooner if I get discharged before then and can land a decent job in Vancouver.

I don't know if I will be able to make it for your wedding Bill. Kathleen and I had planned a trip for that week-end and we have our reservations made. Don't count on me for sure Bill, but if I can postpone the other arrangement, I will drop in to see the knot tied.

I saw Don South this afternoon, and being a wonderful gossip told him of your big date. He expects to have a 48 that week-end and said he would try to get to the church just to lend you a little moral support.

Les was up here last week on his rounds. He was not quite sure but expected to go to Edmonton for the NW staging Units' audit but he might be back in time. He stays with Tom McMurray when he is in town so you could contact him through Tom - Bird and Company - Standard Bank Bldg. Hastings St Vancouver or Arlington Apartments Robson Street. Betty who I saw a couple of weeks ago, is looking good and we spoke about you - nothing good - is staying with her folks at Pat Bay. Godwin is the name.

Bill I must apologise for not answering your letter. But you know the old saying about the way to hell and good intentions. I had your letter on my desk only yesterday but stalled in writing. Also have taken it on two trips to Vancouver intending to write. One of the trips was my annual leave. Had a whale of a good time first three weeks of July. Went to Hope for a few days and then to Savary Island -north of Powell River - for a week and spent the rest of the time between trips in Vancouver with Kathleen. She was on the trips too so you can figure it out that I had a pretty good leave and perhaps not blame me too much for not writing.

There is no chance of a flight for me and I don't care about it. Have lost all interest in the outfit and want only to get that little piece of paper. There is quite a lot of excitement in this regard and a fair-sized quota has just come in. I hope my number is included but don't have much faith.

Comox would be a pretty good station if I did not have my main interest in Vancouver. As it is, I have developed into quite a scrounger of 48s and

72s have been able to get across at least every
two weeks and occasionally an extra one or two.
But am always living in dread that they might
start to get tough. We no longer can fly over so
it makes the trip pretty worrisome besides being
expensive. My girl's name is Kathleen Dunnet and
if you are poking around Hastings West, she works
for Campbell Finance Corporation, do drop in and
say hello to her. She would like to hear from some
of my old pals and I would not like her to see any
one more than you.

Bill, give my best regards to Irene and tell her
that she must keep you well in hand, train you
right from the start and you might turn out all
right in the end and tell her not to forget my
advice on families and best of luck to both of you.

Cheerio Kids,

    be happy,

        Fitz

O.B. ALLAN
LIMITED
JEWELLER AND OPTICIAN
CABLE ADDRESS "DIAMOND. VANCOUVER"

GRANVILLE & PENDER STS
VANCOUVER. B. C.

August 3, 1945.

R 143019,
Cpl. Treadgold, W.O.
R.C.A.F. Station,
Patricia Bay, B.C.

Dear Sir:

In reply to your letter of August
1st, we regret to state that Mr. Boden is in Montreal at the present time. However, he will be back
in Vancouver on August 15th and will give this matter
his immediate attention.

If you feel that this will be too
late, we will be pleased to send you a selection of
rings on approval.

In any case, it would probably be ad-
visable for you to let us know if you wish a plain
gold ring or a diamond set ring. Plain gold rings are
priced from $7.50 plus tax and diamond set rings from
$30.00 plus tax.

Thanking you for your inquiry and
awaiting your instructions, we remain

Yours truly,

O.B. Allan, Ltd.

BA*CS

per. O.B. Allan jr

O.B.ALLAN
LIMITED
JEWELLER AND OPTICIAN
CABLE ADDRESS "DIAMOND. VANCOUVER"

GRANVILLE & PENDER STS.
VANCOUVER, B.C.

August 10, 1945.

R 143019,
Cpl. Treadgold, W.O.
R.C.A.F. Station,
Patricia Bay, B.C.

Dear Sir:

Replying to your letter of August 9th, there will be time when you come to town to choose the wedding ring and look over our stock.

We are pleased to inform you that the earrings are ready.

Thanking you for your past favours, we remain

Yours truly,

O.B. Allan,Ltd.

FH*CS

per...................

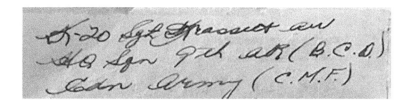

K-20. Sgt. Krasselt A.W.
HQ Sqn. 9 CAR (BCD)
Cdn. Army Overseas

20 Aug 45.

Dear Mr. & Mrs. William Ottley Treadgold: -

Or would you rather me call you just plain Bill and Irene? In any case here's very hearty congratulations to you both and here's wishing you all the very best for many long years of happiness together. Also many thanks for your kind invitation to attend the big affair. Strange as it may seem I received the invitation just about the time you were saying that popular expression "I do", so I marched smartly up to the bar and "bent the elbow" a couple of times in order that you may have good health.

It sure was swell to know that the Jap "do" is a thing of the past. Seems that all the Cdn Army with the exception of the BCD's had a couple of days off to celebrate the occasion. However, we plugged on. Maybe we'll get some time off at the end of the month when the local "square heads" celebrate their Queen's birthday. However, I won't be here 'cause came up Wednesday at 11:30 I'm heading for Paris and 9 days leave. I'm working things pretty these days. Since I last wrote I went on a three-day tour of Germany and after that spent four days in Amsterdam. What a life without a wife — or should I have said that — don't take me wrong.

Well Mr & Mrs I'd better sign off and climb into the "sack". Can't afford to lose my beauty sleep especially with a Paris leave to look forward to.

Au revoir 'till next time with all best wishes and good luck from that guy called

Krass.

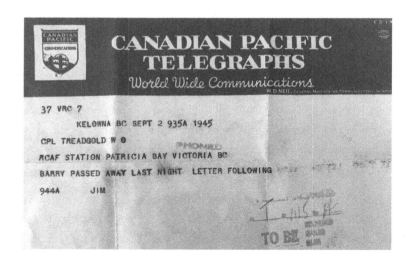

CANADIAN PACIFIC
TELEGRAPHS
World Wide Communications

37 VRC 7

KELOWNA BC SEPT 2 935A 1945

CPL TREADGOLD W O
RCAF STATION PATRICIA BAY VICTORIA BC

BARRY PASSED AWAY LAST NIGHT LETTER FOLLOWING

944A   JIM

Box 62

Kelowna BC

Sunday Sept 2nd, 1945

Dear Bill:-

No doubt my telegram was quite a shock to you and
Irene but that's the way life seems to go at times.

Barry took sick on Wednesday night, apparently
from eating green fruit, and it looked just like a
bilious attack but the diabetic end showed up and
the doctors were not able to balance his system.
He went into a coma on the Friday night and was
taken to the hospital, but never came to, passing
away on Saturday evening. He never responded to
treatment, but went very suddenly, not expected.
At the time as they had every hope he would be out
of it by morning. Violet was on with him at the
time and she took it very hard, says she never saw
anything so quick. Mother has taken it very hard

as expected but others seem not too bad, I will let you know in a few days how things are.

We are getting settled at last and I think we have the permits through for the warehouses so that is at least a start and will give us more room. We should be able to start them in a week or two, providing Dad stands up. He is fine so far but I am a little leery of him, as he may go to pieces yet, but certainly hope not.

Will drop a line in a day or two, hope you folks are getting settled.

    Love

        Jim

S.D. Treadgold
Kelowna
Sept 7th 1945

Dear Irene and Bill

We received your very beautiful letters and much appreciate your kind words. I do not say or write much tonight as my heart is very heavy but I must thank you now. Aunty Annie Treadgold is with us awhile. We have not contacted Frances yet as she is off on leave but hope to soon. She expects to be home about the 15th by her letter yesterday.

We may hear again tomorrow and be able to reach her on her way to Banff.

Barry passed away quickly the darling I loved so much. Some time I will tell you all about it. He

has been so well. The pictures you snapped while
here are grand. We got them today.

Wilma, Thomas, Irene, Uncle Jim Palframan;
Miles, Donna and Barry

The store seemed to be closed when Wilma went to get them. He is really beautiful in all of them. I am afraid it will take me a time to get over this terrible feeling.

Dad has been wonderful under the strain and Wilma has been wonderful too. I think I have been the worst but I have tried and will continue to do so. Jim Palframan left yesterday for the East. He seemed to have enjoyed his holiday.

I will be glad to have Frances if only for a short time. She is being moved from Peregrine. Where she does not know yet. She was in Montreal on the 4th waiting transportation but she was gone to Ottawa or somewhere and the C.P.R. did not seem to find her.

I am so pleased you are comfortable in your cabin and only wish I could drop in. I will write you more when I feel like it. I am too tired tonight.

Sat. 2pm. Wilma is going to mail this for me. I have said very little but will write more again. We have heard nothing of Frances but hope to soon. The flowers you asked us to get we have not been able as yet but may get something and send what is not used. His flowers were nice but had to be made privately. We hope to make his grave beautiful but I am unable to think just now. I hope you are both well and very happy.

The weather has turned cooler but quite nice. Well Bill this is just a line to thank Irene and yourself for the lovely letter. We are all fine so don't worry about us. I will write soon and say more later.

With heaps of love from us all

As ever

    Your loving mother

      Don Treadgold

S.D. Treadgold
Kelowna, B.C.
Sept. 18th 1945

Dear Irene and Bill

Your very kind letters received Bill and very glad to receive them.

Frances came home last Thursday. Jim and Wilma went to meet her. She was indeed shocked as we were unable to reach her.

She leaves a week from today for Toronto where she will be stationed.

Donna has been home from school with a cold but I think she will go at noon today. She wrote a letter to you all by herself. All on her own. And wants me to mail it. The dear has been restless at nights grieving in her own quiet way.

There is so much it is impossible for me to understand the workings, why should one we loved so much be taken. He was truly the sweetest of all children, so loving. It has been the shock of my life. I had done so much but I now wish I had done more and it makes it hard. I may see some day why it "should be". I thought Wilma seemed some better this morning when she got up and left for some work at the store. It is best she should be kept busy. I am glad you are so happy. There is nothing like it. Dad and I did not seem to have much grief and sorrow for so many years but we have had a restless time for awhile. It was a worry but this is a real heartache.

You asked for the pictures but I am not sending them just now. I would not have them lost for anything. They are so grand.

The weather is very nice but was quite cold last night. The days are bright with sunshine. I should get to work as there is lots to be done. I like work when I feel like it.

This is not much of a letter but I wanted to write you so with love to you both

As ever

Mother

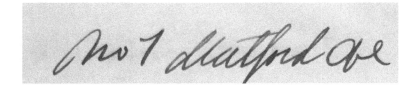

J. Palframan

Sept. 30 1945

Dear Bill

Yours and Irene's letters received and many thanks for the snaps. Well, it is so long ago, I do not just remember what ones I did want! All I am sure of, is one of your Mother and Dad, if you have one, and I would sure be pleased to have one of Irene if you have one to spare.

Bill's parents Sarah Donalda Treadgold and Arthur Thomas Treadgold
with Donna peaking out of the background

Well I am back at the old job again and were they glad to get me back. They phoned several times wanting to know when I would be home and what a mess I ran into. Nearly all new men on the job and no one knew what was wanted or what things were for and I was real busy for a few days getting things straightened out and since then I have been taking things easy and I have been working a week now with a raise in pay and enough pay to take a holiday.

I had a fair holiday in Kelowna and I expect to take another trip back there in about three years if all goes well as well the people out here are not so good.

Wilfred is just out of the hospital after an operation. Millie is taking a couple of weeks holidays as a rest cure and Willo is not so hot. I guess I'm the only well one of the lot.

It is so good to hear that you have a place to live in and not too far from the camp (base).

Well Bill I guess this is all for this time and many thanks for the snaps and if you have real good one of Irene you can send it as I think she is a real fine wife for you and I think she is Just It - so be good to her and use her right! If you don't I will come out there and beat you up and this is not just hot air!

So kind regards to yourself and best wishes to Irene and kiss her one for me.

    Yours Truly

       J Palframan

L.A.C. Gilchrist, K.D
Celle Germany

Oct. 2/45

Well, well, congrats to you two. My but I was
delighted to hear the news and also thank you for
your invitation! I had no idea that you two were
that serious but with me I couldn't keep my own
love straight and so therefore I guess I didn't
have time to watch others. Anyway I wish you all
the Happiness in the world and that all your troubles will come in small bundles!! I envy you Bill
because she's a real fine lady and she shall, I'm
sure make you very happy and to you Dear you sure
picked a winner in Bill.

I've heard from Howard Fitzpatrick who is at
present running Prince Rupert. He sure gets some
awful postings that's his third tour in the bush
and I guess I just cut my ties in time or else I
too would be serving another tour. The last letter
I wrote you would have been from Wundturf but now
that we're here in Celle I suppose this will be
my permanent address. They're all trying to figure
out their Report WOs so far all I can get out of
them is that I'll be home a year from now providing
my record stays clean.

During the latter part of Aug. I spent three days in Amsterdam and enjoyed myself seeing all that I could in adverse weather. I told one cute thing that they needed all the canals to take away the water. She was a good kid so took it good naturedly. This weekend I'll be off to Drave-Mundi "Little Canada" the club is called, it's my first trip there and by all reports it's really the spot – tennis, horseback riding, swimming BRRRR!! – cold now, so I guess life over here won't be too bad. On the 18th I'm off to attend a course in Brussels, there is an educational tour on the interests of the city – they have a similar course in Paris and the arrangements are perfect – tours, shows, gals – Wow!! Invites to homes and dances! The Beaver House will be our home there whilst on the course. Well Love Birds, I'll leave you for now and get back to my work.

Just

Gil

S.D. Treadgold
Kelowna, B.C.

Oct. 3rd 1945.

Dear Irene and Bill

Your letter received today Bill and glad to hear Irene is a little better and will soon be all well again. We are washed up after supper and it is dark. We seem so quiet. It is trying to rain but not very cold, although we need a fire to be comfortable. We had a letter from Winnipeg but Frances will be in Toronto now and hope to soon hear from her. The blues pretty bad at times and things are not the same for me. I find it very trying and wonder sometimes if I will ever feel quite the same again for it is hard to shake but I will have to do the best I can. My nature is not so hard and I still want to remember a lot of my darling. I will never forget so it is not going to be easy for me. At the same time, I don't want to worry others. I think it would be better if I was a little harder like so many.

How do you like the new time? It is light in the morning but quite dark early here.

Dayton Williams died last Sunday rather suddenly and is being buried tomorrow, his son was coming from Toronto so the funeral was held over. They had quite a big golden wedding just a month ago tomorrow. So lots can happen in a month. What a queer world sometimes. It seems that way to me.

Dad has been busy with the new warehouse. He says he is glad to be busy so he can't think. I have done so little this month; work does not appeal to me just now.

Well I have not got this letter off yet. Another day has come and quite nice. Dr. Knox came in yesterday and left me some pills etc and lots of advice. He said to take a holiday which is hard unless we all go. I would not care to go off. It is easier said than done. Time will have to go on I suppose, how much I don't know.

I heard last night that Leonard Wade was killed. I think in a crash or something in the East. Another sad home, what a world this is. One does not help the other carry when it is the ones you love so dearly. The older people are not so bad as the young darling. They are the hardest to put out of your thoughts. They seem to be loaned to us for awhile. I don't want to make this a sad letter but it's simply how one feels and I think best said than not passed off as it is all very real and seems to come to all in turn. Had I have even thought that this was coming it might have helped. It just came so quickly. It is hard for all.

Well Bill don't work too hard as there is always lots of work but don't over due.

Donna is taking lessons and seems to be taking quite an interest. She is a dear and does miss her pal so. She says so little. She and Miles are together a lot but as time goes on she will be more on her own. They go together for lessons.

I may take a walk to the shop to put in time.

Wilma is fairly good but it is not so sharp on her. I was the one so close to him as Dr. Knox says it is better to have loved and lost than not have loved at all which is true, for one's life is much richer but the ache is there just the same, and we must go on, but forget I never will. It will ease off as it must do. I will love and work for the others. Thanks so much Bill for you nice letters and I hope all is well with you now. With love to you both

As ever

Mother

Thanks for the pictures Bill - how lovely

S.D. Treadgold
Kelowna, B.C.

Oct 16 / 45.

Dear Bill and Irene

Well, its hard for me to settle down and write a few lines but here goes - I had a visitor today also two other Air Force men from Kamloops, your old friend Mr. Porter. He called at the shop produced a bottle and we had a very nice chat. He spoke well of both of you and wished to be remembered.

I just answered a letter I received from Ella Thompson (Ella Cameron) asking me to try and have Wilma come down and stay with her for awhile but I told her that Wilma puts me off by saying that Donna needs her here - and she doesn't want to go to Vancouver at the present time but I wish she would go it would relieve Mom as she is still feeling very badly - lost pretty near all inter- est in things it's terrible - it's a pretty hard blow. I feel terrible myself but I have been kept pretty busy what having to look after five paint- ers and the new addition to the shop which is all but finished. Jim and I have been helping as Mr. Cather has other work and is trying to get fin- ished before the weather changes. The new addition is 20x40 ft and when finished will make a splendid warehouse and shop - concrete walls and asphalt rolled floor.

Store fronts of Treadgold Sporting Goods
and Treadgold Paint Supply located at 1619 & 1615 Pandosy St., Kelowna, B.C.

We sure missed Frances when she left - Mom is in such a terrible condition caused by Barry's passing that most anything could happen. I have done my best to cheer her up but it certainly has taken a terrible hold of her she sure is a bunch of nerves - I often wish Frances was back for good her company would certainly help. If Mom could only have some company when we are all away in the daytime it would be wonderful. She says that being alone is terrible I take her for a drive about every other day around looking at jobs or calling on prospective work.

Wilma is down at the shop on book work every day arrives about 9:15 and leaves at 5 PM. but I know she is not interested either in books or banners she seems to feel terrible and I think she misses Barry so but she keeps a stiff upper lip.

Well folks I hope these few lines don't bore you too much and here's hoping you are both in the best of health

Yours

Dad

Treadgold, F.M.
H.M.C.S. "York"
Toronto, Ont.
22 Oct, 1945.

Dear Irene and Bill -

Many thanks for the nice birthday card which arrived on the day. What a good memory you have Bill!

I have been going to write you ever since your wedding day, and now it's nearly the end of October. A good correspondent I'll never be!

Your wedding pictures are lovely - I saw them all when I was home in September. You both look so very happy in every way.

What do you need in the way of household equipment? I would like to send you something useful - something that you haven't already. Be sure to let me know, as if I choose something on my own, as sure as guns I'll pick something of which you have at least half a dozen.

It is wonderful being in Toronto after Halifax. It's clean and bright and the stores are a joy. Clothes are terribly expensive though, and the quality is not of the best – that is compared to what we could get a few years ago. I am trying to get a civilian wardrobe together and have already invested in a two-piece red woolen dress and a black dress with sequin trimming. A hat I cannot find. Anything I put on my head looks "queer" after wearing a tricorne for so long.

When are you going to be demobilized? As for me, it won't be for a while yet as I am busy helping to discharge others. I interview Wrens and male officers as they leave the service and make out a WD12 form on each one. No doubt you know what that is, as all three services use the WD12 which gives the discharges complete history from date of birth to date of demobilization.

The Toronto climate (or something) has made me terribly sleepy. My first week here I just couldn't keep awake. However, each day finds me a little brighter and soon I hope I'll be back to normal.

I have seen Millie and Willo a couple of times. They are both fine and are talking of retiring. At present they are living in an apartment but they would like to buy a small house somewhere not necessarily in Toronto.

Don't forget to send me a list of a few things you would like - then I'll go shopping and see what I can find.

I'm sleepy again!

     Love

          Frances

                    S.D. Treadgold
                    Kelowna, B.C.

                    Nov 1st / 45

Dear Irene and Bill-

Thanks for the cookies Bill. We are enjoying them also your letter today. Dad and Donna are both out again and looking better but Dad still has some cold. It has rained so, I never saw anything like it but today it is clear but not too bright.

Thanks again for your nice letter Bill. You seem to think you know how I feel, well it is pretty awful still. Barry did steal into my heart so I don't think Dad should be so cross, as it does not improve it any. I am not trying to make it worse as it really hurts. I think of so much, men don't feel as women do. It will take a time I know for me to feel as I did. I was so happy with the children and like to do for them. There is not anyone to say a word to, which makes it harder. I can't even think when Dad is around much less mention his name. I don't think lots of these things, for the best, his sweet life never hurt anybody. It is hard to cast it off all at once. Young people can throw things off more quickly and the house is full of reminders. It is best to keep busy I know but that too is not everything as I always did keep busy, perhaps too busy.

The days are going. Time seems to pass in spite of all. Wilma and Harold are going to Jim's for supper tonight. I sometimes wonder that Wilma has not gone much worse I think I should have done. She's quiet and worries I am sure at times I expect I am the one that has had the load and after you can see such a lot we could have done, which does not help. This is surely the sorrow of my life and I must get over it hard as it may be but forget never. It is milder today after a wind storm last night.

I must drop Frances a line. Dad will be writing you I expect. I have very little to write about as I am out so little these days. I don't feel like walking far.

Donna wrote you a letter a couple of days ago and is at me to mail it.

Write soon,

with love to you both

    As ever

        Mother

Dear Bill and Irene
You are still my
sweethearts I hope I
See you Soon Irene
THANK you FOR
The CANDYs.

Patrons:
THEIR MAJESTIES THE KING AND QUEEN

The Canadian Red Cross Society

FOUNDED 1896   INCORPORATED 1909
British Columbia Provincial Division

✚

Red Cross ____ BRANCH
Golwood ____ B.C.
3rd. Nov /45

Cpl. Threadgold. W.
RCaF. Station.
Patricia Bay. B.C.

Dear Cpl. Threadgold:

This is just a little note to thank you for taking such an interest in our case. We received our cheque yesterday, and we both realize that without your help, we would still be waiting this time next year for them to make up their minds.

So, many thanks again for all you have done

Sincerely,

Marjorie & Blake White

A.T. Treadgold

Kelowna, B.C.

Tues night Nov. 7 1945

Dear Bill and Irene

I received your letter re building permits etc. etc. I gave it to Jim to digest - your idea of Irene applying might be alright on the other hand there may be a little difficulty anyway I haven't had time to go into details - my pen has just run out of ink and the bottle is dry so here goes the old pencil - 1st seeing that both Jim and I applied for the present shop addition and as I told you that I had papers drawn up by Don Filmore in Jim's name so I could build across the back of both lots - well we succeeded and Fred Gore the Inspector hasn't been around to pass the job - but expect him any old day now - then what I want to do just as soon as the City seems satisfied is to have Filmore change the Sale agreement in both your name and Jim's- it seems to me that if this were done everything else could stand investigation. I hear that some Government Inspector is expected here soon to go into complaints re home building it seems some people get it all and others get none - anyway Bill we can't do much till Spring and I think in the meantime will get into costs, make a blue print and have everything ready - you might get your discharge before you think then we could get some action but I will get Jim to apply for a trade Licence right away as I believe an application must go to Ottawa to be granted.

Now if you think that I have overlooked any point you just write and say so - as I am liable to be a little asleep at the switch.

Well Irene you will know soon about your discharge - and how it feels to be on the outside and wondering what is next - but don't worry as everything I hope will turn out for the best.

I haven't spoken to Johnstone about the house but will if you are out before the place is ready - Mum and I have talked it over and we intend to insist that you stay with us, so don't worry about that - by the way Bill Mom might be some better but not herself by a longshot, it seems to have shaken the life out of her - she complains having to be left alone all day - and I guess it's quite lonely - I don't know what has got into Alison she hasn't been over for over two weeks and Mum sure notices it I think will speak to Jack - as we cannot understand it - it seems funny since Mike came back she seems different - for weeks she was over 3-4 times a day and to stay away for so long it's hard to understand perhaps I shouldn't have mentioned this but nevertheless I have - things might change even tomorrow and she might be over as usual again -

Bill does Irene intend coming this way after she is out as I am sure Mother would by all she says like it very much but, it's so hard to advise others what to do - as she would be away from you and that doesn't always work out so hot. If I knew when you would be out yourself - it would be quite easy for me to write and say what's trump - but anyway Bill you two will have to use your better judgement and to fit things together to your own advantages.

My cold is still with me but I am working as usual - it snowed a little today and seems quite wintery.

Don is over her cold but is quite deaf - if she doesn't get better soon, I will take her to Dr. Panton as I guess its wax lodged and needs working out - well folks I can't think of any more tonight so best of luck

    Yours

       Dad

          K-20. Sgt. Krasselt A.W.
          HQ Sqn. 9 CAR (BCD)
          Cdn. Army Overseas

          13 Nov 45.

Dear Bill:-

Many thanks for your very welcome letter which I received yesterday. Also for the enclosed snaps. They're really good and you certainly look very happy - but then as the saying goes "that's the way it should be".

Was very sorry to hear of the death of your nephew and also that your parents and sister have been on the sick list. Sure hope that they are all well again by now.

You ask when I'm coming home. Well Bill had I not been one of the "frozen few" I'd have been home some time ago in paints. However, I had to stay with the Regiment - just another penalty a single guy pays in the Army. We expect to leave Holland in mid-December and sail for Canada from England on the Queen Elizabeth on or about the 22nd of January. This will put us home about the 1st week in Feb. Not exactly the best time of year to land home - but believe me - home is going to look mighty sweet regardless of the weather. Come to think of it - it's just four years ago tonight that we stood on the deck of the "Andes"××× and watched the harbour lights at Halifax fade away.

You mention Paris. Well, Bill it's certainly a great place. Mighty expensive - ou la la - what fun. Since then, I've been over to Pilsen & Prague in Czechoslovakia and en route saw a good many of the larger German cities and the Rhine & Ruhr valleys. Friday of this week I'm going over to Berlin, which I think will wind up my travels except of course for the journey home.

Think I'd better sign this off and hit the hay. Was out till 5 this morning at our Armistice dance in the mess. Maybe you'll understand now the reason for the mistakes & scribble.

Please thank Irene for her kind regards and return mine to her. No, not that way Bill - you know me better than that.

Au revoir - with all best wishes & good luck - as ever.

     Krass

B. Johnstone
PO Box 955
Kelowna BC

Nov 18 1945

Dear Bill

Your parcel to hand ok many thanks. The contents will bring a smile to a couple of people we know. Thanks again. We had a short spell of winter which made things most unpleasant, put a lot of telephones out of business, including the phone at the folks, for a few days I understand your Dad found the break near the house and fired it. The weather has moderated now and nearly all the snow has disappeared round town. Your mother is still about the same, I am sorry I cannot say she is any better her nerves are in bad shape. Wilma is about the same sometimes better other times not so good. She was down at my place the other Sunday to dinner. She always enjoys herself playing over my records and going through my cupboards seeing what she can find to chew on. There is no one to check her up every move she makes. It always takes me about an hour to get her to make up her mind to get a move on to get ready to go home. I don't think the folks like her to come round very much. That is too bad as she sure does enjoy herself. I had my picture retaken today Sunday after a good rest. Mr. Ribelin himself came down to the studio (special appointment). If you care I will send one along. My hearing aid is working ok but I don't think I am going to get 180 bucks worth of pleasure out of it. I think it would make a swell pocket receiving set. So, Irene is getting her discharge I guess she is not sorry. I think it would be rather nice if she came down for Christmas nicer still if you can come together. Some time I will be calling on you for some more you know what but I don't think its fair for me to let you pay for them as sooner or later you will be getting your discharge and you will need a stake more than ever now that you are married. Write me soon

With love and best wishes to Irene and your self

      Your old friend

         Bob

               J. Palframan
          No. 7 Stratford Ave

             Dec. 8, 1945

Dear Bill

Your letter received a couple of weeks ago and was pleased to hear from you. Thanks a lot for the snaps. I will get one myself one of those times when the spirit moves me as I have not had a picture taken for nearly 40 years and since then I have got a lot better looking - but not as much since.

Well if I was closer, I would take you up at your word and have a meal from you but I might drop in too often then you would wish I would drop out of sight. Well I wrote a couple of letters to your mother since I came back and have not received any reply from her and as for Frances I have called her a dozen times and left word for her to call me up and I don't know if she received the message or not but she has never called. Elmer was married a couple of weeks ago. Millie and Willo went to the wedding; he was married in Galt. I was not bid, in fact I did not know he was getting married till a couple of hours before.

Well, we are having real nice weather here now like summer lately we had a little snow a week ago but sure have had a lot of rain lately and I think I made a mistake in not staying in BC since I have come back, I have found nothing but lots of hard work but I got a little more money. I am in charge of ½ dozen men here and with them and the cabinet makers fending forth and wanting things and the Boss wanting to know what the hold up is, they would drive you nuts some days. I get fed up and tell them all to go to IT and walk out.

Well Bill, it is nice to know that Irene went to Kelowna for a few days to help your Mother and I think that was real good of her and I expect to take a trip back to BC in two or three years and if you are anyway close I will call on you, then she can wait on me at the table. Well Bill, I hope you can make this writing out I am such a poor hand writer I hate to sit down and write a letter so if you cannot make all of it out you will just have to guess at it as my fingers were not made for writing letters, they are too big and clumsy so I guess I will close for this time hoping to hear from you again soon and thanks a lot again for the snaps so best wishes for Irene and yourself.

J.Palframan

J. Palframan

No 7 Stratford Ave

Xmas Day 1945

Dear Bill and Irene

Just a few lines this time to say I received your parcel a few days ago and thanks for the lovely photo and words fail me to say how much I appreciate it and it makes a swell Xmas gift and if I was close to you so I could drop in I would personally wish you a Merry Xmas and after getting your photo I find that I have a few friends and that my visit to BC was not wasted.

I had a Xmas card from Jim and the family in Kelowna but that is the only word I have had from that part of the country. I have not seen or heard tell of Frances yet but I think she was in to see Millie.

Well we have been having real winter weather here since I wrote to you last. It has been real cold and today it is trying hard to rain. This is what one would call a white Xmas with a little bit of snow on the ground, not very much.

Well Bill this is just a few lines to say I sure appreciate your gift and I think it is a little better than I expected so thank you Irene again wishing you a Happy New Year.

EPILOGUE

And just like that these treasured letters ended.

The war was over and many of Dad's friends returned home to Kelowna. The cherished friendships and unbreakable bonds continued their entire lives. When life allowed (family and work were the priorities) they continued to enjoy their times together - fishing, hunting, a meal or simply a coffee. Dave Chapman even became our older brother's Godfather.

For the Treadgold family, that fateful 1st of September changed everything. Barry's death was the family tragedy they had miraculously avoided during the war. As their friends had done when their children were killed in action, they put on brave faces and did their best. Our grandparents, though, never recovered from their grief; Wilma relapsed and was never again independent; Donna and Miles lost their joyful childhood.

Frances came home first, with Bill and Irene following, and together, like their parents before them, worked tirelessly to ensure their family was well loved and cared for. With kindness and boundless energy, they carried on with our grandparents' core values – education, hard work, honesty, respect – thereby ensuring that future generations would enjoy lives full of confidence, courage and integrity.

Thank you, Dad, for giving us this intriguing perspective. Your legacy continues to inspire us and has brought us even closer together.

"Reading the letters brought back lots of memories, both good times and sad times. So grateful for Uncle Bill and Aunt Irene for all they did for me." ~Donna

"Whatta life!"

Bill doing a swan dive

Bill and Irene and their children.

Enjoying his Civic Duties - Bill as City Councillor and Mayor of Kelowna, B.C.

· My School Chum the Mayor ·

What dreams lie within the hearts of man
   Who dare their best to do :
not content watching others passing by ,
   When they'd rather wear the shoe :
On interest in the wants of others ,
   still time to love your own so dear :
keep up the fight for good and for life ,
   those too few years, we have here :
Take office when it shows its face
   Your time for life is here :
Knock not the ones whose ideas differ ,
   bring them a little near :
Give as before your very best ,
   they will soon advance a cheer :
Wear your gown with all good grace ,
   The voters they are clear :
Show that you are honest as you have done ,
   Good luck the coming year .

· Earl K. Ward ·

A poem for Bill written by Earl Ward

I met some great people in the R.A.A.F. Real friends. Should have kept in touch! Bill Mar/2000

Bill had a wide assortment of hobbies throughout his life ranging from racquet stringing, listening to music to gardening and beekeeping.

Wilma, Bill and Fran 1995 at Bill and Irene's 50th Wedding Anniversary Party

ACKNOWLEDGEMENT

C. Pavlik

Kelowna, B.C.

June 3, 2021

Dear Dad,

Thanks so much for saving your treasured letters. Wendy and I had a terrific time collaborating together to create *Dear Bill*. We felt this project was a labour of love and are so grateful for the experience, even the roller coaster of emotions resulting. Dad, you once again opened doors for us to learn and grow and share a rich history with others. We trust that you are pleased that we were able to make profound connections with the past, and form deeper relationships in the present.

Dad, when you asked Wendy to "do something" with these letters she really took it to heart. It was an absolute pleasure supporting her vision. The unwavering spirit, camaraderie, and knowledge Wendy supplied made teamwork a dream. Dad, we feel your love as we give thanks to all who supported us through the writing of *Dear Bill*. Their encouragement, ideas, and edits, gave us the push we needed to keep us motivated to share the letters in a way in which you would have approved.

We think there will be many valuable discussions and actions resulting from *Dear Bill*, and look forward to being a part of that.

You, your family, your friends, and everyone fighting for fairness and peace, are being honored and remembered significantly.

With love,

Cathie

LETTER WRITERS IN
ORDER OF APPEARANCE

	Name/Vitals	Information	Letters Written
1	Dave Addington Chapman November 25, 1919 November 7, 1975	No. 635940. A.C.; 25 Squadron "E" Flight; Royal Air Force Dave was the youngest of 4 children born to David and Jesse (Haynes) Chapman. (Joyce-1913; Eric-1916; Philip-1917; David-1919) Seeking adventure he left Canada at the age of 19 and travelled to England to enlist in the Royal Air Force where he became a crew member of a Lancaster Bomber crew and saw action in Britain and Africa during WWII.	2
2	WG Jaggard		1
3	Sarah Donalda Treadgold June 7, 1883 February 14, 1963	Sarah Donalda Treadgold-Daughter of John Palframan and Frances Wheeler; born in Erin, Wellington County, Ontario Canada. Siblings: James W, Annie E, Amelia Maud, Wilfred John, and Willo. She married Arthur Thomas Treadgold 29 March 1906 in Guelph, Ontario and promptly moved to Kelowna, having their first of five children, Frances Muriel Treadgold Oct.17, 1907.	58

	Name/Vitals	Information	Letters Written
		"Sarah Donalda Treadgold was an active and conscientious volunteer who understood the value and importance of working for the community. She was deeply interested in education and initially volunteered for many years on Kelowna Elementary School's P.T.A. She was encouraged to run for the office of school trustee in 1924 and topped the polls in every election for the next 23 years. Sarah was a loving mother with good ideas and the passion to stand up for what she believed - much like the other women who have been and will be honoured with the Sarah Donalda Treadgold Citizen of the Year Memorial Award" (City of Kelowna, Fred Macklin and Sarah Donalda Treadgold Memorial Award - citizen of the year, 2021).	58
4	W. Sydney Dawson		1
5	Frances M. Treadgold October 17, 1907 October 25, 1998	Born in Kelowna B.C. First child of Arthur Thomas and Sarah Donalda Treadgold. Accomplishments: 1924 age 17 - teacher at a one room school house in Red Deer; 1925 Grade Two teacher Kelowna, Central Elementary;	4

	Name/Vitals	Information	Letters Written
		1933-34 Leave of Absence from SD #23 to teach in Ontario; 1942-46 military service with the Women's Royal Canadian Naval Service WRCNs working up to Lieutenant; 1946-1957 Primary teacher, 1957-59 SD #23 Teacher Consultant, 1959-1968 SD#23 Supervisor. Quote from January 5, 1968 article by Terry Utley in the Kelowna Courier: "There are hundreds of young people in Kelowna who owe their educational start either directly or indirectly to Miss Treadgold."	
6	James (Jim) Slater Treadgold March 14, 1914 February 6, 1986	During WWII Jim worked in anti-aircraft in a gun factory in Vancouver, making machine guns for airplanes. After the war Jim and Bill ran Treadgold's Sporting Goods together from 1946 to approximately 1966. Jim was a professional gunsmith, superb mechanic and professional rifleman - he put scopes on everyone's rifle and tested them out. A really good hunter - big game hunter. Jim was an upland game hunter too. He was very good with his hands (notes from interview of Bill by Cathie Pavlik, 2008).	4

	Name/Vitals	Information	Letters Written
7	Wilma Gwendolyn Miller (nee Treadgold) October 1, 1910 February 17, 2001	Wilma was well loved/supported while living with the consequences of the medical decisions made for her. Growing up, Wilma excelled at school, enjoyed writing poetry, dancing and having fun.	2
8	Arthur Thomas (Tom) Treadgold April 5, 1889 June 4, 1957	Born in Paris, Ont. and died in Kelowna B.C. Arrived with wife Donalda in Kelowna in 1906. Thomas, an active citizen, was an athlete, artist, painter, decorator and owner of Treadgold's House of Decoration on Pandosy Street. Treadgold's paint and signmaking shop was a Kelowna fixture for many years.	5
9	Arthur John (Jack) Treadgold April 10, 1912 April 15, 1988	Jack was a talented musician, painter, house decorator, hunter, horseman, hunter and gardener. Following WWII Jack was co-proprietor (with his dad) and then sole owner of Treadgold's Paint Supply. He was an active citizen and a Kelowna city councillor between 1951 and 1963 (notes from interview of Bill by Cathie Pavlik, 2008).	2
10	Rep from Royal Bank of Canada G.C (signature illegible)		1

	Name/Vitals	Information	Letters Written
11	Rep from Royal Bank of Canada F.T. Willis		1
12	Alban W. Krasselt February 18, 1918 January 8, 2005	H.Q. Squadron 9th Armoured Regiment (BC Dragoons) Canada Alban was born in Edmonton and moved several times before settling in Kelowna at the age of nine. He was a good student and enjoyed sports and especially fishing with his friends. After finishing school he went to work for the CN railway, doing various jobs, including loading boxcars. After the war he returned to Kelowna, again working for the railway, working his way up to become the shipper. In 1948 he married the love of his life, Sarah Gage (Sally). They raised three children and continued to enjoy fishing and camping. Alban moved to Sun-Rype Products where he worked for 22 years as the Traffic Manager. During his retirement he attended several world war commemoration ceremonies in both Holland and Italy. He remained an active member of the BC Dragoons and attended many reunions with his fellow veterans (Bev Sperling nee Krasselt, personal communication, July 2021).	26

	Name/Vitals	Information	Letters Written
13	Arthur Treadgold April 2, 1856 October 6, 1948	Born in Warwick, Warwickshire, England and passed away in Vancouver B.C. Lived at the "Firs" Theatre St. Warwick in 1882. Occupation gardener at Warwick Castle. Credited with developing certain Delphiniums. Married Harriet Atkins 02 May 1882. First child, Helen Mary Treadgold b 07 Apr 1884 Paris ONT, Canada. "My grandfather was 94 when he died. I visited him at the hospital in Vancouver – he'd had a stroke and never got over it. In the Fraser Valley he had a tree with six different kinds of apples on it. He was a horticultur-ist – he learned in England. He married a Canadian woman – she had a brother who had the first house in Glenrosa [Kelowna] – in the 20's" (Notes from interview of Bill by Cathie Pavlik, 2008).	1
14	Phillip Hayne Chapman October 29, 1918 February 25, 1941 Age 23	L.A.C P.H.C., R/92341, #7 S.F.T.S Son of David and Jessie M. Chapman Kelowna BC; husband of Eldith Chapman, Vancouver.	2

	Name/Vitals	Information	Letters Written
15	Ernie Alexander 1918-?	Ernest Archibald Alexander Rank: Squadron Leader Unit: No.1 Service Flying Training School Awarded Air Force Cross on: January 1st, 1945 "This officer is an exceptional pilot and instructor. His efforts as senior examining officer and squadron commander have contributed very largely to the high standard of pilot training carried out by his unit. His perseverance and capable supervision make him a model flying instructor. His outstanding ability and devotion to duty are praiseworthy and an inspiration to the pupils and instructors under him" (TracesOfWar.com, May 20 2021).	2
16	Doug Monteith	CAN. R97951 RCAF Overseas. No.500 Squadron, Aux. Airforce	3
17	Doug Alexander	MPO #1303	1
18	Tom Noble	R118464, AC2	1
19	Earl Ward	Can R 118309	3
20	J.H.Bowes	Lawyer Chilliwack, B.C. Probably a relative (Grandfather?) of Alvin and Marguerite Bowes who were mentioned by Krasselt. 22 illegible letters.	26

	Name/Vitals	Information	Letters Written
21	Bill Arthur		1
22	Frances J. Henderson		1
23	John (from Penticton)		1
24	Harry Bell October 8, 1920 November 13, 1996 4 Anti Tank Regt. R.C.A. C.A.O.	Joseph Henry Thompson (Harry) Bell was born in Lethbridge, Alta. The eldest of five siblings and loving son to Doris Daisy Bell b. 6 April 1893 d. 03 May 1977 and Joseph Bell b. 23 April 1882 d. 21 Jan. 1931. When Harry was stationed in England during WWII his cousin (Harry's Dad's twin's son from South Africa) was passing through London (he was stationed in England too) and immediately realized they were related. They had corresponded and knew they would be in the same area at this time so had hoped they would meet for the first time then. They never met again and no pictures were taken (Irene Treadgold nee: Bell, personal communication, 2000). Before the war Harry worked for Disston Saws in Vancouver, B.C. Harry was married in 1950 to Eleanor (nee Dick) and soon after that the company moved him to Seattle where they raised their family and resided for the rest of their lives (Morgan Stewart, personal communication, July 2021).	1

	Name/Vitals	Information	Letters Written
25	Leon Elmer Gutpell 1912-1987	R.C.N.V.R. (Navy) Leon was Bill's cousin.	1
26	Willo Palframan June 25, 1897 - ?	Willo was S.D Treadgold's sister and known to family as always happy, a joker and content.	1
27	E.A. Porter	No. 15 X Depot, RCAF, Kamloops, B.C.	2
28	Cpl Flude J.H. (Harry)	RCAF R.128476	1
29	K.D. Gilchrist	RCAF R.144505	2
30	Sgt. J.J. Fitzgerald	RCAF R.142602	1
31	J. (Jim) Palframan 1883 - ?	We believe this writer was Bill's uncle (Sarah Donalda's brother). Jim was born in Guelph Ontario, was a carpenter and built coffins (notes from interview of Bill by Cathie Pavlik, 2008).	2
32	Bob Johnstone	Bob was a bachelor and a great friend of the Treadgold family. He worked for A.J. Boatworks and lived on Abbott St. in Kelowna, B.C.	1

FOOTNOTES

i   **Royal Tour Across Canada** in May, 1939 cited torontoPubli-clibrary.typepad.com

ii   http://www.thepeoplehistory.com › 1939. Cited May 24, 2021

iii   **1939 - Mac Colville, Neil Colville & Alex Shibicky** New York Rangers "Bread Line". The Rangers' top line, known as the "Bread Line" was Neil Colville at center, his brother Mac at right wing, and Alex Shibicky at left wing. The line played together coming up through the many ranks of the Rangers' system, and they proved to be the team's bread and butter, thus earning their nickname.

Neil Colville / Mac Colville

Born in Edmonton, Neil and Mac Colville played with the New York Rangers, winning the Stanley Cup in 1940. During the war, the brothers were stationed in Ottawa and played on the army's Ottawa Commandos team, winning the Allan Cup in 1942.

After the war they returned to the Rangers as defensemen, the first pair of brothers to do so in the NHL.

Alex Shibicky

Was a crowd-pleasing forward team known for his Fierce Attacks. Best known for being the first player to use a slapshot, which he did in 1937.
Spent three years in the Canadian Forces during World War II.

Phil Watson: born Montreal April 24, 1914

1938-39 – NHL Most Game Winning Goals (7)

1939-40 – NHL Stanley Cup Champion
1941-42 – NHL Most Assists (37)
NHL Second All-Star Team
1943-44 – NHL Stanley Cup Champion

Later took the Rangers to the playoffs in three of his four seasons as a coach in the 1950's. Cited: Alex Shibicky; Phil Watson; Neil Colville / Mac Colville: Wikipedia May 20 2021

iv   **Sarah Donalda Treadgold** served on the Kelowna School Board for 23 years. Cite: **City of Kelowna** Fred Macklin and Sarah Treadgold Memorial Award May 20 2021

v   **Timeline Second World War** thecanadianencyclopedia.ca cited May 26, 2021

vi   **Redhill** - 1937 saw the RAF Volunteer Reserve (RAFVR) establish a training school at Redhill, which was operated intensively up to and during the Second World War. Redhill became a fighter base with Spitfires stationed during the period of the war. It was home to Canadian and Polish squadrons and acted as an advanced airfield for the attack on Dieppe in August 1942, housing some 800 personnel at the time. March 17, 1940 Dave Chapman post: Cited Redhill Aerodrome Wikipedia, the free encyclopedia May 20 2021

vii   **The East Coast Fighter Command**: *(Dave Chapman post):* was a formation within the RAF and played an important role during the Second World War. Its most important contribution was the protection of Allied convoys from attacks by the German Kriegsmarine's U-boats. It also protected Allied shipping from aerial attacks by the Luftwaffe. The main operations were defensive, defending supply lines in the Battle of the Atlantic, as well as the Mediterranean, Middle East, and African theatres. It operated from bases in the United Kingdom, Iceland, Gibraltar, the Soviet Union, West Africa and North Africa. It also had an offensive capacity. In the North Sea,

Arctic, Mediterranean, and Baltic, strike wings attacked German ships carrying war materials from Italy to North Africa and from Scandinavia to Germany.

The Command saw action from the first day of hostilities until the last day of the Second World War. It completed one million flying hours, 240,000 operations and destroyed 212 U-boats. Coastal Command's causalities amounted to 2,060 aircraft to all causes. From 1940-45 Coastal Command sank 366 German Transport vessels and damaged 134. Total tonnage sunk was 512,330 tons and another 513,454 tons damaged. 10,663 persons were rescued by the Command, comprising 5,721 Allied crew members, 277 enemy personnel, and 4,665 non-aircrews. 5,866 Coastal Command personnel were killed in action. Cited RAF Coastal Command: Wikipedia May 20 2021.

viii   **Wireless Operators** Wireless operator/air gunner – The role was to send and receive wireless signals during the flight, assisting the observer with triangulation "fixes" to aid navigation when necessary and if attacked to use the defensive machine gun armament of the bomber to fight off enemy aircraft. Cited RAF Bomber Command aircrew of WWII - Wikipedia

ix   **Canadian Forces Base Borden** (also **CFB Borden**, French: **Base des Forces Canadienne's Borden** or **BFC Borden**), formerly RCAF Station Borden, is a large Canadian Forces base located in Ontario. The historic birthplace of the Royal Canadian Air Force, [2] CFB Borden is home to the largest training wing in the Canadian Armed Forces.[3] The base is run by Canadian Forces Support Training Group (CFSTG) and reports to the Canadian Defence Academy (CDA) in Kingston. During the Second World War, both **Camp Borden** and **RCAF Station Borden** became the most important training facility in Canada, housing both army training and flight training, the latter under the British Commonwealth Air Training Plan (BCATP). The BCATP's No. 1 Service Flying Training School (SFTS) was located here until 1946. Relief landing fields were located at Alliston and Edenvale. A third landing field, known locally as Leach's Field, was operated by Camp Borden from the 1920s to the 1950s. The L-shaped airstrip was rudimentary; the "runways" at Leach's Field utilized the existing ground surface. It was primarily used for touch-and-go flying. Cited: CFB Borden: Wikipedia

x   **Oct. 2 / 41 William Andrew Cecil (WAC) Bennett** - won the British Columbia Conservative Party's South Okanagan 1941 nomination and the election for the Provincial Legislative Assembly. Following the election, the Conservative and Liberal parties voted to henceforth govern in coalition, an arrangement formally titled the British Columbia Coalition Organization. As a coalitionist, Bennett was re-elected in 1945, but vacated the seat in 1948 in order to run, unsuccessfully, as Progressive Conservative candidate in the Yale federal by-election of that year. Regaining the Coalition nomination for the South Okanagan seat, Bennett was returned to the British Columbia Legislative Assembly in the 1949 provincial election. After failing in his bid to become leader of the provincial Progressive Conservative Party in 1951, he left the party to sit as an independent member. In December of that year, he took out a membership in the Social Credit League. Cited: W.A.C. Bennett: Wikipedia

xi   **Initial Training** RCAF– *(Ernie's letter Nov.23/41)* One of the first and most important contributions our country (Canada) would make to the war effort would be the British Commonwealth Air Training Plan (BCSTP) in which Canada agreed to provide facilities and training for airmen from every part of the Commonwealth. Canada was ideally suited for this program because our country was far from most of the active fighting and had lots of wide-open spaces and good flying conditions.

Training was challenging and rigorous. Pilots, wireless operators, air gunners, and flight engineers went through months of training at specialized schools.

Of the Canadians trained in the <u>BCATP</u>, 25,747 would become pilots; 12,855 navigators; 12,744 wireless operators; 12,917 air gunners, and 1,913 flight engineers. Cited: Initial Training; veterans.gc.ca

xii   **Operation Drumbeat** uboat.net cited May 30, 2021

xiii   **9th Armoured Division – B.C. Dragoon** (Krasselt)

Battle Honours

Liri Valley; Melfa Crossing; GOTHIC LINE; Pozzo Alto Ridge;

Lamone Crossing: Naviglio Canal; Fosso Munio; Conventello-Comacchio;

Italu, 1944-45; Ijsselmeer; Delfzijl Pocket; North-West Europe, 1945

The Final Phase: Securing Northwest Europe

The way was now clear for the final phase of the campaign in northwest Europe. On March 23, Field Marshal Montgomery's Allied forces began the assault across the Rhine. Although the First Canadian Army did not take part in the crossings, the troops of the 9th Canadian Infantry Brigade, under British command, participated in the crossing of the Rhine at Rees. In this operation a Canadian medical orderly, F.G. Topham, earned the Victoria Cross for his heroic care of a wounded man. Cited:B.C Dragoons Canadian Armed Forces April 2021

xiv   **No. 500 (County of Kent) Squadron AAF** was a Royal Air Force flying squadron. (Doug Monteith) It was initially formed in 1931 as a Special Reserve squadron and in 1936 became part of the Auxiliary Air Force, at this time based at Manston and Detling.

During the Second World War, the squadron served in both Coastal Command and Bomber Command. In the coastal role, the squadron undertook operations over the English Channel in 1940–1941, before moving to North Africa in late 1942. It undertook anti-submarine operations in support of Operation Torch and then continued operations in the Mediterranean, operating various aircraft types during this period. In July 1944, the squadron disbanded before being reformed as a bomber squadron in Algeria in August, later operating in Italy in the final years of the war. Following the war, the squadron was disbanded in October 1945. Cited: No. 500 (County of Kent) Squadron AAF Wikipedia April 2021

xv   **RCAF Coal Harbour** - The townsite and surrounding area was the site of a Royal Canadian Airforce base for seaplane patrols in the Northern Pacific during World War II. Many of the original buildings still remain, such as the general store (the old gymnasium), and the officers' barracks immediately overlooking the harbour. RCAF Stranraers and later Canso-As (the Canadian designation for Consolidated PBY Catalina flying boats built by Canadian Vickers) were based here. Anti-aircraft ordnance, ammunition storage for depth charges and considerable concrete fortifications were built. A Stranraer was lost with all its crew during the war in mysterious circumstances.

There is a small, free museum dedicated to the RCAF station built and maintained by a private individual in the sole remaining Canso hangar. Cited: Coal Harbour: Wikipedia May 2021

xvi   **The Canadian Ordnance Corps** was redesignated the Royal Canadian Ordnance Corps on 29 Apr 1936. In the Second World War, the RCOC had a strength of 35,000 military personnel, not including the thousands of civilian personnel employed at RCOC installations. They procured all the material goods required by the Army, from clothing to weapons. Up until 1944, the RCOC was responsible for maintenance and repair. Ordnance Field Parks, that carried everything from spare parts to spare artillery, supported the Divisions and Corps. Cited: The Canadian Ordnance Corps; Wikipedia; April 2021

xvii   **Currie Barracks** The Canadian Army opened what was called the **Currie Barracks** on the southwestern edge of Calgary in 1933, occupying a property on the level plateau above the south slope of the Bow River valley. The facility was named after the recently deceased General Sir Arthur William Currie, commander of the Canadian Expeditionary Force on the Western Front during World War I. Cited Wikipedia May 2021

xviii   **Krasselt entry – April 26, 1942** *The Dancing Years* is a musical with book and music by Ivor Novello and lyrics by Christopher Hassall. The story takes place in Vienna, from 1911 until 1938. It follows the life of a penniless Jewish composer and his love for two women of different social classes, set against the background of Nazi persecution. Cited: *The Dancing Years* Wikipedia April 2021

xix   **No 151 Wing (Earl Ward reference) Royal Air Force** was a British unit which operated with the Soviet forces on the Kola Peninsula in the northern USSR during the first months of Operation Barbarossa, in the Second World War. Operation Benedict, the 1941 expedition to Murmansk provided air defence for Allied ships as they were discharging at ports within range of *Luftwaffe* units in Norway and Finland, then converted Soviet air and ground crews to British Hawker Hurricane IIB fighters and their Rolls-Royce Merlin engines, many of which were due to be delivered under British Lend-Lease arrangements. 1940-41: Army cooperation (aircraft - Lysanders / Tomahawks) 1941-42: Tactical reconnaissance, home based (Mustangs) 1942-45: Ground attack and tactical reconnaissance North Africa and Italy (Hawker Hurricanes) Cited: **No 151 Wing** Wikipedia March 2021

xx   **No 214 Squadron** *(Earl Ward reference)*: Inverness the Canadian Ordnance Corps was redesignated the Royal Canadian Ordnance Corps on 29 Apr 1936. In the Second World War, the RCOC had a strength of 35,000 military personnel, not including the thousands of civilian personnel employed at RCOC installations. They procured all the material goods required by the Army, from clothing to weapons. Up until 1944, the RCOC was responsible for maintenance and repair. Ordnance Field Parks, that carried everything from spare parts to spare artillery, supported the Divisions and Corps. Cited: No 214 Squadron Wikipedia March 2021

xxi   **RAF Ferry Command:** *(from Earl Ward's letter – Jan1/43 referring to his brother Bill Ward; and Phil Chapman 29-4-42):* was the secretive Royal Air Force command formed on 20 July 1941 to ferry urgently needed aircraft from their place of manufacture in the United States and Canada, to the front line operational units in Britain, Europe, North Africa and the Middle East during the Second World War. It was later subsumed into the new Transport Command on 25 March 1943 by being reduced to Group status. Cited: RAF Ferry Command Wikipedia March 2021

xxii   During the 1930s, many psychiatrists in Europe and North American began experimenting with new forms of treatment for the mentally ill. The introduction of new forms of treatment began an era of new therapies in psychiatry, including the use of insulin coma, electro-convulsive therapy (ECT), and psychosurgery to treat patients with various mental disabilities. https//sencanda.ca

In British Columbia, these treatments were widely employed across all of the mental institutions after 1942. Recently, historians have shown that women patients at Essondale and the Provincial Hospital for the Insane were more likely subjected these harsh treatments (Sterilization, insulin therapy, ECT, psychosurgery) than their male counterparts. Cited: www.arpnbc.org<ay 20 20221

Riverview Hospital - From the opening in 1913 to 1959, a series of new buildings were designed and opened on the property to accommodate the demanding growth and advancement of mental health in BC. The Boys' Industrial School was constructed in 1920 to allow a safe place for troubled juveniles to be morally rehabilitated. The Acute Psychopathic Unit was opened in 1924 to test treatment methods and assign treatment plans to new admissions; today this building is called Centre Lawn. 1930 brought about the opening of a female patient building called the Female Chronic Unit, and known today as the East Lawn Building. This 675-bed facility enabled most of PHI female patients to transfer to Essondale. It also opened the doors for the first psychiatric nursing training school in BC to begin. Other disciplines that followed were occupational therapy and social work. The Veterans' Unit was opened in 1934, and in 1949, the second half of this building was completed; entirely renamed as the Crease Clinic of Psychological Medicine. The Crease Clinic functioned as an acute hospitalization unit for voluntary patients to be admitted and treated; allowing people to voluntarily seek help was a key step in recognizing mental illness on the same level of importance as physical illness. Cited: Wikipedia March 2021

xxiii　**Type 1 Diabetes in Children** - Symptoms of type 1 diabetes in children can start very suddenly. The exact cause is unknown but in most people with type 1 diabetes, the body's immune system — which normally fights harmful bacteria and viruses — mistakenly destroys insulin-producing (islet) cells in the pancreas. Genetics and environmental factors appear to play a role in this process exposure to various viruses may trigger the autoimmune destruction of the islet cells.

The symptoms may appear very quickly and may include:
- Increased thirst
- Frequent urination, possibly bed-wetting in a toilet-trained child
- Extreme hunger
- Unintentional weight loss
- Fatigue
- Irritability or behavior changes
- Fruity-smelling breath

Type 1 diabetes may cause sudden, extreme swings in blood sugar that can be dangerous. If you notice any of the symptoms of diabetes in your child, it's important to get them a physical exam as soon as

possible, so their doctor can begin treatment right away. Cited: Mayo
Clinic March 20 2021

xxiv   **The Halifax VE-Day** riots, 7–8 May 1945 in Halifax and
Dartmouth, Nova Scotia began as a celebration of the World War
II Victory in Europe. This rapidly evolved into a rampage by several
thousand servicemen, merchant seamen and civilians, who looted the
City of Halifax. Although a subsequent Royal Commission chaired by
Justice Roy Kellock blamed lax naval authority and specifically Rear-
Admiral Leonard W. Murray, it is generally accepted that the underly-
ing causes were a combination of bureaucratic confusion, insufficient
policing, and antipathy between the military and civilians, fueled by
the presence of 25,000 servicemen who had strained Halifax wartime
resources to the limit. Cited: The Halifax VE -Day Wikipedia March 2021

xxv   **June 1945 - RMS *Aquitania:* *(Gil Gilchrest)*** was a British
ocean liner of the Cunard Line in service from 1914 to 1950. She was
designed by Leonard Peskett and built by John Brown & Company
in Clydebank, Scotland. She was launched on 21 April 1913[5] and
sailed on her maiden voyage from Liverpool to New York on 30 May
1914. Aquitania was the third in Cunard Line's grand trio of express
liners, preceded by RMS Mauretania and RMS Lusitania, and was the
last surviving four-funnelled ocean liner.[6]

Shortly after *Aquitania* entered service, World War I broke out,
during which she was first converted into an auxiliary cruiser before
being used as a troop transport and a hospital ship, notably as part of
the Dardanelles Campaign.

The company planned to retire her and replace her with RMS *Queen
Elizabeth* in 1940. However, the outbreak of World War II allowed
the ship to remain in service for ten more years. During the war and
until 1947, she served as a troop transport. She was used in particular
to take home Canadian soldiers from Europe.

After the war, she transported migrants to Canada before the Board of Trade found her unfit for further commercial service. Aquitania was retired from service in 1949 and was sold scrapping the following year.

Having served as a passenger ship for 36 years, *Aquitania* ended her career as the longest serving Cunard vessel, a record which stood for six years until overtaken by RMS Scythia's service record of 37 years. In 2004 Aquitania's service record was pushed into third place when *Queen Elizabeth 2* became the longest serving Cunard vessel. Cited: RMS Aquitania Wikipedia March 2021

xxvi   **Bergen-Belsen** *(Gil):* Approximately 50,000 people died in the **Bergen-Belsen camp** complex. Among them was Anne Frank, the most well- known child diarist of the Holocaust era.

As Allied and Soviet forces advanced into Germany in late 1944 and early 1945, Bergen-Belsen became a collection camp for thousands of Jewish prisoners evacuated from camps closer to the front. The arrival of thousands of new prisoners, many of them survivors of forced evacuations on foot, overwhelmed the meager resources of the camp.

At the end of July 1944 there were around 7,300 prisoners interned in the Bergen-Belsen camp complex. At the beginning of December 1944, this number had increased to around 15,000, and in February 1945 the number of prisoners was 22,000. As prisoners evacuated from the east continued to arrive, the camp population soared to over 60,000 by April 15, 1945.

From late 1944, food rations throughout Bergen-Belsen continued to shrink. By early 1945, prisoners would sometimes go without food for days; fresh water was also in short supply.

Sanitation was incredibly inadequate, with few latrines and water faucets for the tens of thousands of prisoners interned in Bergen-Belsen at this time. Overcrowding, poor sanitary conditions, and the lack of adequate food, water, and shelter led to an outbreak of diseases such as typhus, tuberculosis, typhoid fever, and dysentery, causing an ever-increasing number of deaths. In the first few months of 1945, tens of thousands of prisoners died. Cited: Wikipedia March 2021

xxvii   **Western Air Command** was the part of the Royal Canadian Air Force's Home War Establishment responsible for air operations on the Pacific coast of Canada during the Second World War. Cited: Bergen-Belsen Wikipedia May 20 2021

xxviii   ***Moonlight and Cactus*** is a 1944 American musical western featuring <u>The Andrews Sisters</u>. The screenplay concerns a ranch owner whose cattle are stolen. Cited: Moonlight and Cactus Wikipedia March 20 2021

xxix   **Halifax Explosion**: The **Bedford Magazine explosion** was a conflagration resulting in a series of explosions from July 18 to 19, 1945, in Bedford, Nova Scotia, Canada. During World War II, the adjacent cities of Halifax and Dartmouth, provided heavy support for Canada's war effort in Europe.

Not long after VE-Day, on the evening of Wednesday, July 18, a fire broke out on the jetty of the Bedford Magazine, now CFAD Bedford (Magazine Hill) on the Bedford Basin, north of Dartmouth. The magazine fire began when a barge exploded that evening at 6:30 PM, quickly spreading fire to the dock where ammunition had been temporarily stored outside due to overcrowding in the main compound. A chain reaction of fires, explosions and concussions ensued, continuing for more than 24 hours. Cited: Bedford Magazine explosion Wikipedia March 2021

xxx   The **RMS Andes** was built in Belfast in 1937–39 and completed at the outbreak of the Second World War. The Admiralty almost immediately requisitioned her as a troop ship and had her converted to carry about 4,000 troops. In troop service she broke three speed records for long-distance voyages. https://en.wikipedia.org/wiki/Troopship July 19 2021

ABOUT THE AUTHORS

WENDY HAMILTON

The third child of Bill and Irene Treadgold, Wendy loves making plans and having adventures.

Following in her Aunty Frances' footsteps Wendy pursued a career in education, working as a classroom teacher (elementary and primary), Learning Support teacher, Special Education Coordinator /Case Manager, Counselor and coach (track and field, field hockey). During this 37-year span Wendy and her husband raised three delightful children in different B.C. locals where a lake, a ski hill, tennis courts and a golf course were always close at hand.

Currently residing in Balfour B.C. with beautiful views of Kootenay Lake and the Selkirk and Purcell Mountain Ranges, Wendy is living her retirement dream with her husband Dennis (Milt) of 45 years – travelling, golfing, boating, skiing, gardening, socializing with friends, and grand-parenting their amazing 7 grandchildren.

Carpe diem!

This is Wendy's first foray into book writing.

CATHERINE PAVLIK

Cathie Pavlik, the fifth child of Bill and Irene Treadgold, was born and raised in a special time in Kelowna, B.C. Cathie was fortunate to be given a wide variety of learning opportunities which serve her well to this day. After attending Kelowna Secondary School and competing in many sports, she left her hometown as one of the first women to receive a full athletic scholarship (field hockey) at Washington State University, where she obtained her Bachelor of Science in Physical Education (Minors in Health and Business).

Following university, Cathie became a devoted teacher and coach at KLO Secondary/École KLO Middle School in Kelowna for 35 years. She advocated for individualized learning practices as well as developed and supported initiatives for healthy lifestyles in and outside the school. Cathie and her husband, Dave, also raised their two wonderful children, and when their kids went to university, Cathie obtained her Masters of Science in Education at the University of New England. Now in retirement, Cathie enjoys spending time with her grandchild, friends and family, volunteering, taking courses, skiing, boating, travelling, gardening, and having that second cup of coffee at her leisure.

Cathie lives by the motto "work hard, have fun, be safe."

CPSIA information can be obtained
at www.ICGtesting.com
Printed in the USA
BVHW071304151121
621608BV00001B/1